THE
FALLEN
STONES

PREVIOUS TITLES BY DIANA MARCUM

The Tenth Island

THE FALLEN STONES

CHASING BUTTERFLIES, DISCOVERING MAYAN SECRETS,
AND LOOKING FOR HOPE ALONG THE WAY

DIANA MARCUM

Little
a

Published by Little A, New York

www.apub.com

Amazon, the Amazon logo, and Little A are trademarks of Amazon.com,
Inc., or its affiliates.

ISBN-13: 9781542022859 (hardcover)
ISBN-10: 1542022851 (hardcover)

ISBN-13: 9781542022835 (paperback)
ISBN-10: 1542022835 (paperback)

Cover illustration by Naveen Selvanathan

Cover design by Faceout Studio, Tim Green

Printed in the United States of America

First edition

Raise up your glass and
Revel while it lasts

—"End of the World," Drew Holcomb &
The Neighbors

AUTHOR'S NOTE

If I read a book with a note at the beginning stating some facts have been changed, I'll spend the rest of the time wondering if so-and-so really had curly hair or if there was a house in such a place or if that person really said that thing.

So let me say that some facts have been changed—with the caveat that none were essential facts. Small details about people met in passing have been changed to protect identities since neither I nor they planned on them popping up in this book. Some names have been changed and some identities concealed to protect the guilty. Everything else I have tried my best to get spot on.

—dm

One

The Very Bad Vacation

As a girl, any time I'd pick a library book, I'd flip through each option, skimming the story, and put the book back on the shelf if it began with a couple who was already together. What was the point of reading anything without a budding romance?

So I'm loath to mention Jack Moody right at the start. But we were already a couple—on the verge of breaking up, should that add any intrigue—when we discovered Belize and the butterfly farm that would come to obsess me.

We often joked that our relationship was like an arranged marriage. We had known each other forever without romantic inclination. He was the divorced, single father of two who lived down the street. A photojournalist at the same paper where I was a writer. Several other Jacks worked there (hence my newsroom habit of using his last name). I found him cranky. He considered me flighty.

Then one summer, after his kids were grown, after we no longer worked at the same paper, we fooled around and fell in love, as the Elvin Bishop song goes. Despite our personality quibbles, we could vouch for the other being basically decent, and anyone who has dated enough knows that's nothing to scoff at.

It wasn't until after I'd moved to an island in the middle of the Atlantic that Moody had an epiphany and called to say "I love you." I found his timing suspicious, considering I was six thousand miles away. He flew from California to the Azores islands twice, and we, being older and attempting to be wiser, negotiated the relationship as if we were two families haggling over the number of goats to be exchanged. Once we settled our negotiations, we congratulated ourselves on our fine matchmaking skills. We liked recalling incidents of prior disinterest. That time I'd been planning to break up with a doctor and Moody had said, "But he's a catch and he doesn't even mind the way you laugh." How I had tried to set Moody up with my single girlfriends, telling them, "He doesn't say much, but he's handsome if you like that standard astronaut, baseball-player kind of face from back when those types all looked the same." It was a sweet and easy-breezy arrangement until I landed a journalism fellowship at Harvard.

For me, the fellowship was a chance to right an ancient wrong. I had not gone to college when deep down I believed I was destined to be a scholar. This was an opportunity to fix that—at Harvard, I might become the kind of person who could readily locate countries on a map, accurately define the waves of feminism, and really *get* photosynthesis. And just the idea: Harvard. I'd never dreamed they'd let me nose around there.

Moody liked the idea of leaving our California home and spending a year on the East Coast. He wanted to go to baseball games at Fenway Park, eat pizza with a crust that drooped off both sides of his hand, and photograph unfamiliar terrain.

We packed up our two dogs and moved to Cambridge.

But my idea of the fellowship turned out to be a "Martian Taco." My friend Michael Mayhew (alliteration demands the use of both names) coined this concept back when we were teenagers. He used it to defend his inexplicable love of Jack in the Box tacos, a disgusting concoction at a fast-food chain:

A Martian Taco

Imagine someone described a taco to a Martian who had never actually seen one: a crunchy, folded edible container filled with something soft and greasy and savory, topped with crisp green stuff and dairy-like shreds and a drizzle of sauce.

The Martian then comes back with a Jack in the Box taco, which matches the literal description while bearing no resemblance to an actual taco. The trick, MM said, was to appreciate it, like he did, as its own entity. It was important to remember all interpretations are based on previous experiences.

I was the Martian at Harvard. I had based my expectations on descriptions and interpreted them as someone who had never actually sampled higher education.

The literature for the fellowship had promised intimate conversations with leaders in many fields. I had conjured up shooting the breeze with scientists, mirth-filled riff sessions with the literati. I was very excited by the new close friends I was about to make. I hoped some of them would own beach houses.

In real life, a staff member entered the room and rang a little bell when we were supposed to take our seats in the audience. Should you wish to ask a question of that day's prestigious guest, you were to introduce yourself with full credentials in the manner of a White House briefing.

Spouses and partners of fellows were known as "affiliates" and strongly encouraged to take part in seminars. It was "our" fellowship year, we were told.

The year began with a two-and-a-half-week, eight-hours-a-day orientation that covered everything from the correct way to wear a bicycle helmet to the history of Harvard's statuary. It featured testimonials from former fellows.

One of these fellows advised us to make time for something fun. During her fellowship year, she told us, she had not only studied statistics, conflict, and Israel but had also enrolled in a soul-stirring poetry class, learned Croatian just because, and taken advantage of a Harvard discount to rent a scull and row on the river at five o'clock every morning.

"I'm out," Moody told me that night. "This can be your thing. I'll find other ways to keep busy. I'll take the dogs to the park."

"What are you talking about?" I asked. "We can't get intimidated."

"I'm not intimidated," Moody said. "No one should learn to speak a Slavic language just for fun. It's gross. And I'm not a *joiner*. You're the one they want. I'll do my thing. You don't mind?"

It wasn't a question. It was a directive.

He went to the park. He took day trips to New Hampshire. I grew ever more unhappy as I clumsily negotiated the treacherous group dynamics.

I would report back, trying to pinpoint why I now had social anxieties.

"The French writer who never talks to me hates me and I don't know why," I told him.

I recounted the story to Moody: I was finishing writing my first travel memoir and had been discussing a chapter with a friendly colleague when the French writer joined us and asked, "Did you know I also wrote a book?"

I replied, "I'm sorry. I didn't know. But that's wonderful! What's it about?"

"It's about a journalist who *died*," she said, and glared at me.

"Her eyes were like daggers," I told Moody. "I'd been talking about the chapter where my dog eats all the neighbors' bread."

"You're being paranoid," Moody said.

"You had to have been there. Which you never are," I muttered to myself, climbing the stairs to our room while he stayed on the couch.

It snowed. At first, it was magical, leaving icy stars in the eyebrows of George, the shaggy stray we'd brought back from the Azores, and giving Murphy, our lab, an added challenge to his habit of sniffing out food dropped on sidewalks. The snow lured Moody and me out for nighttime walks on silent, glowing streets. Those walks were the first time we had spent much time together since I'd started attending required functions—which was a classification of events that translated to parties without raucous laughter or spontaneity.

It kept snowing. The once-pristine drifts blackened with city soot, their color matching the dingy gray sky.

One afternoon at the fellowship house, a young woman from India and a man who was born and bred to Canadian winters exclaimed from quite different but equally shocked perspectives how cold it was. They were overheard by the curator, who suggested that perhaps they should have done more research before moving . . . to Boston.

Both fellows panicked, worried that they had not sounded suitably grateful for the Harvard Experience. An unsettled tension fell. I wanted to be back in California.

Soon after that, a distinguished journalist told me that I could have been among the best journalists of my time if only—and she stumbled as the unspoken words typed silently out between us—"if only you weren't you."

I told Moody that, in the end, it had come out as, "If only you weren't—you, uh, you—would *you* like more tea?" But the intention was clear.

"Ha! You coulda been a contender," he said, showing off his Brando imitation. "Why are you being so insecure?" he asked. "Why didn't you just ask her what her problem is with you?"

"Why would I want to know something like *that*?" I exclaimed. "Why aren't you on my side?"

"I am," he said. Then he paused. "But I am going to leave for a bit. This weather is getting to me. All of this is getting to me. It's like you joined a cult. You don't mind if I go back to California in a couple of weeks and hang with my brother?"

Again, it wasn't a question. It was a directive.

The next two weeks in our Cambridge rental, we were overly polite, which is our way of being mean to one another. I envy those tempestuous types who battle it out. The conflicts of the mutually emotionally contained are sneaky and draining.

One morning, we made a nice breakfast (or at least as nice as one can make when there are no decent avocados available).

"You can take breakfast with you if you want, since you're always rushing out the door," Moody said.

"Like I have any choice," I said.

"Like you have to go to the coffeehouse? Like you have to go out for drinks with the fellows?" he asked in a mildly curious tone.

"I'm not eating these eggs," I said evenly. "You make rubbery eggs."

Well, after that blowup, all bets were off. When he left for his trip, I said, "So, have fun."

He said, "Take care of yourself. And the dogs."

Clearly, the relationship was in trouble.

The snow piled higher. It got even colder, although that didn't seem possible.

On yet another charcoal-hued afternoon, I was studying beneath three blankets and two dogs—Moody doesn't like the dogs on the bed, but, hey, he wasn't in our bed. He was in California.

The phone rang. I sighed—the photo on the screen was Moody and me in the Azores, back when we were happy. I almost didn't pick up. But I worried that, following that impulse, any universal judge of character might deem me petty.

"Hey, there," I said with false cheer.

"Listen," he said. "Things have been weird between us. I have an idea. Would you like to go to Belize for winter break?"

"Sure," I said. "Where is Belize?" (My geographical inadequacies remained.)

I studied up. Belize is a slender strip of a country, with one foot in the Caribbean and one in the Central American jungles. It is bordered to the north by Mexico, to the south and west by Guatemala, and to the east by the Caribbean Sea. English is the official language because it was once British Honduras, making it the only English-speaking country in Central America. It has the world's second-largest coral reef and a string of cays and white-sand beaches.

It should have been a wonderful vacation. But I am probably not the first to discover that a plane ticket doesn't fix a relationship. One night in a little village next to the ocean, we were lured off course from a seaside stroll by the sounds of an R&B band. The song brought us to a bar where people danced on a dance floor and danced on the sand, writhing to the music. We sat there. I had my eyes glued to a boisterous group of locals, willing them to make contact. Soon, I started chatting with a woman restaurant owner. Her Canadian Jamaican husband good-naturedly invited me to dance. He was the one keeping the party lively, and he knew how to move. I was midgroove when, out of the corner of my eye, I saw Moody storm off down the beach.

When I caught up with him, he yelled, "That was so disrespectful. Dancing with someone else right in front of me!"

For weeks, as I muttered about him leaving me to face "our" fellowship year alone, he'd apparently been stewing. He'd convinced himself that I needed a partner who relished repartee at functions. Someone who liked to do things like . . . dance.

Looking back, I can think, *Poor Moody.* But at that moment, I was as angry as I have ever been. I despise men who try to control women with their little fits and jealousies.

"What's wrong with you? Don't try to tell me what I can and cannot do!" I screamed, no longer envying tempestuous types.

"Maybe you should go find a Diego, a Mikhail, a *Pierre* who likes to daaaaaaance!" he bellowed, doing some odd imitation of a cha-cha-cha. "Maybe you'd be happier without me. Maybe we shouldn't be together."

I didn't think I was the histrionic type, but apparently I am. I started crying.

"Leave me alone. Don't follow me," I hissed and ran down the beach to our sad little shack that he'd booked because he only looks at the photos and doesn't read 227 comments.

When he came in, I slid to the far side of the bed with my back to him, refusing to speak.

I had been happy living on my own before we got together. He'd lured me into this partnership with his trips to the Azores and his general decency. I'd very slowly started to feel a sense of security. Now—boom, it was done, over.

The next morning, he got up early, went for a drive, and saw a keel-billed toucan. I panicked that my passport was with his and he had it hostage. I was going to need it to catch a plane. I was going back to California.

But I'd sublet my California house and he'd sold his. I didn't have anywhere to live except Cambridge. Plus, I'd taken leave from my reporting job at the *Los Angeles Times*. I couldn't just pop back in and tell them Harvard wasn't my thing. A person was only allowed to feel gratitude for cold, glittery Harvard. And the dogs! How would I get them back to the West Coast? How could I have let my life get so entwined with another person's?

Moody came back from his bird-watching jaunt with apologies and breakfast. *Too late,* I thought. He looked at me closely.

"What's wrong?" he asked with alarm. "You look funny."

"You broke my heart," I said. "How am I supposed to look?"

"But you look weirder than that," he said.

I was tired—so tired. And strangely warm, and my skin felt raw. Later that day, a rash appeared on my side.

Moody thought I had an infected sand flea bite. The pests had already gnawed my ankles to a red pulp. He insisted we go to a pharmacist.

We slowly walked our bicycles to town, not speaking. The pharmacist looked and said it wasn't a bite.

She sent us to a doctor, whose one-room office was a few blocks away. The sign on the door said "Dr. D." accompanied by a picture of a stethoscope forming a smile and a phone number. We called the number, and Dr. D. came to the office. He looked at my side. He told me that I had a disease sometimes called "serpent of fire" in Belize. It is also known as shingles.

Shingles? I might as well have packed slippers for the retirement home. *What next? Rickets? Scurvy?*

The fellowship didn't provide health insurance. If I'd gotten sick in the United States, I would have been in dire straits. Luckily, we were in Central America, so I had access to health care. The bill for the medicine and doctor's visit came to forty dollars.

Over the next days, Moody brought me fresh pineapple juice, cool cloths for my forehead, and paperback novels borrowed from a nicer hotel. Dr. Internet informed me that it could have been worse. I could have suffered neurological damage, I could have lost my sight.

The illness was believed to be brought on by stress, so, obviously, Moody had almost blinded me, although I did give him a few small points for his generous care of the afflicted. I had no choice but to let him be nice to me as I convalesced.

A week later, I was back to normal, other than a deep fatigue and a discolored midriff. We left the shack and arrived at Hickatee Cottages, a modest eco-resort in the Toledo District of Southern Belize, where we'd planned to spend the last few days of our trip. That night, we sat on the veranda of our pretty jungle bungalow listening to the whoop-whoop-whoop of howler monkeys in the distance.

"We need to talk," Moody said, which, I knew, was never a good sign.

"I was an idiot," he said. "I have jealousy issues that have nothing to do with us. I'm going to deal with them the second we get home.

"I want us to stay together. I love you. When I'm thinking straight, I know you love me. But we're going to fight sometimes, and you can't start divvying up the dogs every time."

None of those books I used to borrow from the library had a suitor who promised fights.

He nudged my shoulder with his shoulder.

"Will you dance with me? Are you up to it?"

He had a song on his phone, ready to go.

It was Al Green's "Let's Stay Together": *Loving you whether, whether times are good or bad, happy or sad.*

I danced with him, but only after reminding him to be careful not to touch my rash.

Two

The Butterfly Farm

By early afternoon at Hickatee, the air hung hot and still. We'd left the ocean breeze behind. Moody was in the shower, cleaning up. A wrong turn on a jungle hike had left him scratched and bloody. I was in the main house checking emails on my phone (and hiding from blood-thirsty insects).

Alli, Hickatee's owner, was nearby working on her computer.

She had round hazel eyes with long spiky eyelashes, thin arched brows, and a wide smile. Her hair was pulled into a tidy bun, but she had the right kind of face, I thought, for a jeweled headband and bob. Maybe an ostrich feather. She would have made a great flapper.

A year and a half earlier, she told me, she had been a corporate manager in charge of compliance and trainings. She lived in suburban Texas with Eduardo, her engineer husband, and their sons, Jorge and Little Eduardo.

The family decided to take a vacation to Belize mostly because there was a direct flight from Houston. They loved the howler monkeys' chatter at night and the fresh pineapple that arrived by the truckload, and the ocean.

When they returned home, Alli and Eduardo started noticing the preteens in their neighborhood who were obsessed with video games, disconnected from nature, neurotic, and materialistic. Their sons were only a few years away from that future. They decided their main goal in life was to allow Jorge and Little Eduardo to stay children for as long as possible and to keep them from ever, at any age, exhibiting the aforementioned traits.

Online, they found a British couple who was selling Hickatee Cottages. The off-grid property had jungle trails, six bungalows with hardwood floors, and a restaurant/bar with a wide veranda that was surrounded by wild orchids. Two black-and-white cats, Pinto Mis and Boox Mis, were thrown into the deal. (*Mis* is "cat" in Kekchi—also known as Q'eqchi Mayan.)

They bought the place. They quit their jobs, sold their belongings, uprooted their sons, and moved to Belize.

"Of course, we talked it over," Alli told me. "But we were afraid we'd talk ourselves out of it if we went over all the what-ifs too long."

They were still sorting out how to run a hotel when an agitated British millionaire turned up on their doorstep. Clive Farrell was a philanthropist/environmentalist/lepidopterist and owner of the Stratford Butterfly Farm, the largest butterfly exhibit in England, and the Fallen Stones Butterfly Farm, the largest butterfly breeder in Belize.

He explained that the previous owners of Hickatee Cottages were also the business managers for Fallen Stones, helping to get butterflies shipped from the rain forest to Stratford-upon-Avon. He said that if Alli and Eduardo didn't continue with this arrangement, many families in the Mayan village of San Pedro Columbia would lose their livelihoods.

The stakes seemed high. Alli and Eduardo agreed to take on the butterfly farm. They had one stipulation: Eduardo wanted to let their hotel guests visit the butterfly breeding farm—which was closed to the public. He thought the access would give the Hickatee hotel a unique value in the market.

Moody and I were guests, and it was Thursday, the day that Eduardo traveled up the mountain in his truck to visit the farm and bring back the pupae they'd ship out to exhibits around the world. I ran to fetch Moody.

Eduardo drove the three of us north on the Southern Highway, exiting at a town called Dump. We passed through the Kekchi Maya village of San Pedro Columbia with its rounded hills, thatched-roof houses, and seemingly endless population of free-roaming chickens. I marveled at red-pink bougainvillea towering higher than the tallest palms, and watched women in colorful skirts doing laundry at the river. After about a forty-minute drive, we finally turned up a steep, deeply ravined dirt road, where even with four-wheel drive, the tires spun and the truck slid and the three of us bounced around the cab.

I was astonished to see a man on a fixed-gear bicycle pass by us. He had a canvas bag strapped across his chest, full of leaves.

When I stumbled off the roller coaster of a ride, I audibly gasped. We were at the top of the hill on a flat, round clearing. Eduardo pointed west toward pale-blue peaks in the distance. "Guatemala," he said. A quarter turn, and we looked out over San Pedro Columbia and, beyond that, to the blue Caribbean Sea flecked with green. To the north, a vast valley of rain forest lay thick and dark and impenetrable.

He'd parked the truck beneath a flamboyant tree dripping scarlet-orange flowers. In front of the truck, a staircase cut into the earth, led down. The steps looked like they were made from the stones of a Mayan ruin.

Sebastian Shol, the farm manager, greeted us. He had a wide face with a slash of straight black eyebrows. It was a very serious-looking face, which made it even better, months later, when I would watch for the slight smile to twitch across his mouth after he made one of his deadpan jokes.

We followed Sebastian down the zigzagging stones and along a trail. Damp, fragrant leaves squished beneath our boots.

The "farm" he showed us was a series of wooden sheds on stilts scattered among trees and flowering vines where men counted tiny butterfly eggs and changed the leaves in wooden boxes full of caterpillars. Near the sheds were tall wire pens full of fruit and flowers and butterflies. At one pen, Sebastian told Moody and me to slip in quickly, closing the door behind us.

Immediately, we were covered with yellow butterflies. They landed on our hair, perched on our noses, and fluttered past our eyelashes. They were so light, their presence was a bare tickle. We took photos, laughing, and had to pick butterflies off our clothing before we exited the pen.

Another flight cage held brilliant blue morphos—three times bigger than the yellow butterflies with wingspans of about six inches. They flew in lopsided loops, drunk from sucking up rotting mangoes and limes—their favorite food. When they rested, their closed wings exposed an intricate pattern of browns and golds that suggested the watchful eyes of predators.

Our presence in the cage set off a chain reaction, a rippling. Most of the butterflies opened their dazzling wings and took flight. We were surrounded by iridescent blues and violets brighter than blinking lights. The human brain perceives color faster than almost anything, faster than shape or movement. It's a neurological process—we're wired for color, and I felt a surge of electricity as if I were plugged into an electrical current.

I heard Moody say, "Amaaaaazing!" and turned, figuring he was kidding, using an exclamation he insisted I overused. But Moody hadn't been saying it in jest. He was looking up in genuine awe.

The blue morphos' colors are so intense that bush pilots have reported seeing their flashes from the air. The emoji on your phone really doesn't do a blue morpho justice.

That unbelievable color comes not from pigment but from an intricate structure—thousands of shiny scales arranged in a diamond pattern, each with ridges and grooves that act as tiny prisms and mirrors. They disrupt visible light, bouncing back only the wavelengths that humans perceive as shimmering blues. Architects have been studying the blue morpho wing structure hoping that structure might hold the key to an energy-efficient system of cooling buildings, or maybe entire cities.

We couldn't stay long at the farm. The Stratford Butterfly Farm in England had sent their order for Belizean butterflies for that week. Their main customers were zoos and public gardens, or sometimes a Russian oligarch with a thing for butterflies. Occasionally, there would be a request from a bug wrangler on a movie production.

At Fallen Stones, we watched as the farmworkers finished filling the order by gently packing pupae in a wooden box. They had carefully recorded the day each egg had hatched and when each caterpillar had hung from a twig and started to curl into a chrysalis. Inside the chrysalis, the caterpillar turned to liquid, and out of that soup of DNA, a butterfly somehow formed. Each delicate pupae had to be shipped precisely in time or it would emerge en route and die.

We needed to get back into the truck with our ticking cargo. The pupae would travel from the farm to the one-room airport in PG (no one who lives in Belize calls it Punta Gorda) to Belize City, clear customs in Houston and again in London, then journey on a truck to Stratford-upon-Avon where they would divvy up the box and send out the individual orders. The entire trip could take more than a week, the whole time a metamorphous unfolding.

Moody and I followed Eduardo up the ancient stones, life teeming around us. Wild butterflies quivered on matching flowers, bees buzzed, birds called, a flower-scented breeze ruffled the leaves in this sanctuary.

In the truck, rattling down the steep hill, I took Moody's hand— one of the first times I had been the one to reach out since our fight. The wonders of the natural world have a healing influence.

We had a few spare minutes to stop by Lubaantun, the nearby Mayan ruins, and still get to the airport in time. In modern Maya, the name "Lubaantun" translates to "the place of the fallen stones." It was where the butterfly farm got its name. The stone steps at Fallen Stones had come from the ruins at Lubaantun before they'd been protected.

We were the only visitors at Lubaantun. Appolinario, the ranger accepting our foreigner fees at the ruins, bore a strong resemblance to Sebastian. He was, it turned out, Sebastian's nephew. We walked on the long expanse of grass that was once a ball court for *pok-ta-pok* (or *pitz*), a game played with a rubber ball by the ancient Maya.

The Spanish colonizers had never seen rubber before they arrived in South America. It's believed the Maya added spring to the heavy ball by mixing latex with juice from morning glory vines. I mentally added bounce to the list of their achievements in mathematics, engineering, and calendars.

The sun slanted in golden sheets over the tumbled ruins that dated back to about 700 CE. In the deep stillness, there was a feeling that this place reached further back than I had the courage to follow. We all walked our own routes into the hush. It was odd to be experiencing timelessness in a hurry—I could soon see Eduardo waving that it was time for us to go.

That night, after we successfully delivered the box of pupae to the airport, I started thinking about stillness—how freezing is often either our way of trying to hold on to a moment or to escape one. We hold still to stop time and savor a first kiss or to register unexpected danger.

Is that why Lubaantun, which felt so outside of time, had seemed to hold such a quiet stillness? Why was it paused? What was it holding on to? What was it anticipating?

In bed, monkeys howling in the distance, I started reading an excerpt of the *Pooul Vuh*, a text recounting the myths and history of the Kekchi Maya, and there it was, stillness: the one thing that existed before the world did:

This is the account of when all is still silent and placid. All is silent and calm. Hushed and empty is the womb of the sky.

These, then, are the first words, the first speech. There is not yet one person, one animal, bird, fish, crab, tree, rock, hollow, canyon, meadow, or forest. All alone the sky exists. The face of the earth has not yet appeared. Alone lies the expanse of the sea, along with the womb of all the sky. There is not yet anything gathered together. All is at rest. Nothing stirs. All is languid, at rest in the sky. There is not yet anything standing erect. Only the expanse of the water, only the tranquil sea lies alone . . . All lies placid and still and silent.

Three

THE LAST GNOMES OF GREAT BRITAIN

Back at Cambridge, I tried to make up for my previous wallowing. The fellowship had given me a chance to make friends among a group of people I would not normally have met. How often does that happen once you're settled in a career and have a longtime inner circle? There were individuals to treasure in the group, and many of them were soulful and down to earth in a way I hadn't previously given them credit for. A few more rounds of dissecting the pros and cons of the electoral college as if rehearsing for Sunday-morning news shows seemed a small price to pay.

Each day, the walk from my house to the fellowship house took me past the Peabody Museum of Archaeology and Ethnology. The Peabody had sponsored an excavation of Lubaantun in 1915, and inside the museum, there were *pok-ta-pok* ball court markers from the ruins— Appolinario, the Lubaantun ranger, would not approve of what he'd consider their theft.

In Harvard Yard, there were tall casts of late-Classic stelae intricately carved with Mayan imagery and the faces of ancient rulers. I always paused a moment as I walked past to take in their incongruity in this place. Especially when the Mayan gods or rulers wore caps of snow. I signed up for an undergrad class on the Maya and devoured the textbook and materials, even if I was too claustrophobic to attend lectures in the cramped classroom with high, small windows. Those ivy-covered buildings looked more enticing from the outside. With an intensity I had once saved for concert listings, I scoured the list of talks at the Harvard Museum of Natural History for anything on butterflies. Belize and Fallen Stones had sparked something within me, and my interests were still burning.

I often called Janet, my oldest friend, as I navigated the East Coast. We'd been close since our early teens. Back then, we were both daughters of poverty who were bound and determined to live some other kind of sparkly life. We had turned out to be just ourselves, a journalist and a horticulturist, neither destitute nor glamorous. But we retained our shared side hobby of trying to figure out the markers of social class in America. So I, of course, had to provide her notes from the live demonstration at Harvard. I was also always asking her the names of flowers that I'd seen in Belize and had begun to see in Boston gardens as spring arrived.

Moody was no longer leaving for California at every opportunity and even rounded up Harvard fellows to go to a Red Sox game. We were back on good terms, but there was still a vulnerability to the relationship that hadn't been there before our fight. Boston had showed us that we could fall apart—providing the humility required in a long-term commitment. I attended a wedding once where the officiant said that monogamy wasn't about staying in love with the same person but falling in and out of love with the same person many times over. At the time, I'd felt sorry for his wife, who was standing next to me. Now, I think he may have been onto something.

When it comes down to it, there is no *staying* anything in life. It's all transitions. One day, I was a young, single woman. Then "young" was no longer the appropriate signifier. Now, I was adapting to no longer being single, an identity I had long carried, sometimes with frustration and sadness, sometimes with glee and a determination to remain so.

Moody had been a contentedly married father. Then a bitter divorcé. Now, he was starting over with me, and I could see how he might sometimes mix up injured feelings from the past with our present. "Then" and "now" trade places at such a dizzying rate. The only hope is to find the things that hold true when the whole universe, including you, is in flux.

The school year ended, and we packed up the dogs and drove west. Somewhere around Wyoming, Moody asked me what I was thinking of doing next.

I had plans to visit our friend Kari in London and, I told him, I might extend the trip. Before I could finish, he interrupted: "And go find Clive the butterfly guy."

I looked at him, astonished, and he laughed. I'd been thinking about Clive since Alli had described him showing up at Hickatee's doorstep.

"Do you know how many times you've talked about butterfly farms since we got back? When are you going to figure out that I know you, Marcum?

"I think it's a great idea," he added.

Six months later, I was at Clive's estate outside Dorset, a small village in the English countryside. He had offered to walk me through his wildlife sanctuary, and he was upset that the forecast called for rain. It always surprises me when English people are bothered by rain—England is not a land known for endless sunshine.

"In nicer weather, the fields would be dancing with blue butterflies," he said. "I wanted you to see them."

Clive was a compact man in his seventies with a short silver beard and an air of both mischief and a slight sorrow. He was wearing a bucket hat and carrying a walking stick.

On our way out, he loaned me a pair of the Wellies that seemed to be kept on hand for guests with feet of all sizes. We walked along what Clive said was the world's longest buddleia hedge. He explained that the nectar from its spiked violet blooms was perfect for butterflies getting ready to hibernate.

The fields were a carefully restored natural habitat, a tangle of milkweed, perky yellow blooms of horseshoe vetch, the round poms of purple devil's bit scabious, and other butterfly buffet-line favorites. This wild landscape stood in stark contrast to any formal English garden or rolling countryside that had been denuded of wildflowers and pollinators by single-crop farming.

We walked along a dirt path that cut through the fauna and came to a tiny cottage tucked into a hillside. Gray-green rosettes of stonecrop carpeted the roof as if the hills were trying to claim it as their own. I would have missed spotting the weathered door if not for its border of decorative seashells.

We ducked to clear the doorframe because, as Clive explained, this was Dodder's house—and gnomes are short. I had a lot to learn.

No one was home. But there was a candle on a workbench and some crumbs scattered around. The windows were round and covered with cobwebs. Clive told me he'd once had a disaster when a confused cleaning woman had swept away the curated webs.

Back outside, Clive pointed out an exquisitely carved gnome that sat on a deck smoking his pipe. At about four feet tall, he had a long nose, deep-set sad eyes, pointy ears, and a magnificent beard. His peg leg was attached to an acorn kneecap.

This was Dodder, one of the last gnomes of Great Britain, from *The Little Grey Men* by B. B., a book Clive had loved as a child. Clive explained that the gnome's leg had been bitten off by a fox, and that he was sitting and waiting for his brothers to return. Dodder had apparently been waiting fifty years.

"He's the only one left. He's all alone. Poor chap," Clive said.

Farther on, past a stand of apple cider trees, a dragon statue curled along a crest of a hill. Her snout alone was taller than a person, her winding back big enough for a class of kindergarteners to use as a climbing gym. (Schoolchildren did visit the estate monthly.) The dragon seemed sculpted from gray stone, but her scales shimmered green. Dragon eggs sat among long grasses and clumps of Scotch broom.

The rain held off as we walked on to the Island of Dreams, a circle of green surrounded by wildflowers. On the island, there was a towering giant's bed, a well, and a ladder.

"That's where you go to dream. And people dream about water and the underworld, so we made a well for people to look into the murky depths," Clive said. I had heard about the Irish and their fairy trees, but this was a step beyond.

He pointed to the ladder reaching into the sky. It seemed to stretch on forever because the rungs grew ever narrower before disappearing at the top.

"It's a golden ladder to reach the silvery moon," he said, matter-of-fact.

I had been expecting exactly none of this. Clive leaned on his walking stick and looked at me shyly.

"As a small child, I was a dreamer and read every book full of imagination," he said. That was the one thing about this whole situation that I probably could have guessed.

As we continued walking, Clive pointed out plants and real-life creatures with the same wonder as he did the fantasies he'd created.

"Look at this pond! It's a seething mass of life—the dragonflies and the damselflies, and it's the perfect habitat for the great crested newt!" he cried.

He spotted butterfly eggs on leaves, as clear and tiny as drops of water. He turned over leaves to watch the perfectly camouflaged caterpillars eat. His eyes tracked ants and birds and he trilled out the names of the constantly passing butterflies: "Oh, look! A silver-washed fritillary."

It began to rain, but it hardly mattered. Clive was curating a wonderland. It worked in all kinds of weather. But I did understand his disappointment about not being able to show me the blue butterflies because they validated his entire undertaking and underscored unexpected connections between living things.

Clive's team had returned the rolling hills to grassland and planted kidney vetch, with its clusters of yellow flowers sitting atop wooly pads. It's the host plant for the small blue, a tiny dusky-blue butterfly, and now a colony of them fluttered about every year.

They had also planted endless mounds of horseshoe vetch, which also had yellow flowers, in the hope of luring the Adonis blue. Its population had mostly disappeared from England as farmers stopped grazing sheep and its habitat became overgrown. But they were making a comeback, and Clive longed to see clouds of the glittering sky-blue males, and the females, which are a warm chocolate brown with orange and blue accents. So far, he only had them in penny numbers, he said with a sigh.

The Adonis blue lays single eggs that are flat discs on the top of horseshoe vetch leaves in sunny spots, so the egg is almost impossible to see (except to Clive, who pointed one out).

When the egg hatches, the caterpillar is green with short yellow stripes and blends seamlessly into the dark-green undersides of the leaves. The caterpillar is protected by camouflage—and also by an unlikely ally, ants. The caterpillar secretes a sweet, sticky substance that is nectar of the gods to both red and black ants. They "milk" the caterpillars by tickling them with their antennae. While the caterpillar is growing up, it has a constant bodyguard of ants. The ants even sometimes bury groups of caterpillars at night in chambers connected to ant nests, apparently for protection. When the caterpillar pupates, the ants continue to guard it for weeks until the butterfly emerges. This is one of many examples of butterfly-ant symbiosis, even though ants are usually a butterfly predator.

That night, I called Moody to tell him about Dodder and the dragon, along with the giant queen ant and the tree nymph and the blue butterflies, and all the rest of it.

"You know that house in our neighborhood with the miniature cobblestone bridge and the wildflowers and woodland creature statues?" I asked. "Well, it's like that, only if they had a hundred acres and could hire Imagineers."

If Clive had been a rich man who just got really into butterflies, I wouldn't have been so fascinated. Rich people have to find something to do with their time and money. It had all seemed to make sense to me before I visited.

But I had gotten it backward when I'd been dreaming up the story of a wealthy butterfly benefactor. At a young age, Clive had decided he needed to become filthy rich so he didn't have to bother with anything other than butterflies.

He could trace his passion to a specific event. As a child of six or seven years old, he'd found a hairy caterpillar crossing the garden path.

It was "one of those magic childhood moments which we all have, especially if, like me, we have a happy childhood; and then later on, consciously or subconsciously, we look for it again," he told his local newspaper in a 2016 article, which had not adequately prepared me for meeting Clive.

The son of an RAF pilot in World War II, he grew up with modest but comfortable means in a family of nature lovers in the British countryside. Clive worked hard, but on the day of the exams, he panicked at the thought of a future spent in offices and quit law before he began.

Instead, he and a friend started flipping apartments in London, borrowing money and working around the clock. They became friends with a dentist who drove a Jaguar and lived a glamorous lifestyle. The dentist joined their venture, bringing some needed capital. By the early eighties, Clive had become a real-estate development mogul.

About this time, Clive's older brother, a veterinarian, was called to the estate of the Duke of Northumberland to tend to an ailing iguana. Clive's brother introduced him to the duke. A short time later, Clive rented estate lands from the duke upon which to build the London Butterfly House.

Clive took out massive loans to build greenhouses full of exotic plants and butterflies. It was a gamble, something that had never been done before. He didn't know if the butterflies would live, or if captivity in those numbers would set loose a butterfly pandemic. He didn't know if the butterflies would fly around inside the greenhouses. He didn't know, if they did live and fly, if people would come to see them.

He was putting his newfound fortune at risk, but his glitzy London life felt empty. He wanted to do something meaningful, and what held meaning for him was butterflies.

One day, when he was feeling particularly tense about his gamble, the phone rang. It was Dame Miriam Rothschild, the banking-family heiress, the world's foremost authority on fleas, and an expert on a startling array of creatures and plants.

She had heard about Clive's project, and she wanted to know what he was setting out to do and how she could help. She invited him to visit her at Ashton Wold. Her father, Charles, had chosen the site of the family estate in Northamptonshire for its abundance of butterflies.

Clive remembers driving down a long, narrow lane and coming upon the country house completely overgrown with climbing roses, ivy, wisteria, and clematis.

"It was as if it was disappearing into the forest," he said.

Miriam Rothschild greeted him wearing her trademark purple headscarf, loose-fitting clothes, and rubber boots, as she did not approve of animal leather. (She had even worn rubber boots to Windsor Castle.) She was surrounded by a half dozen Shetland sheepdogs.

Clive found himself telling the famously direct woman that he was nervous about the grand scale of his butterfly project.

"Nonsense," said Miriam Rothschild, who, in her life, had done a great many things that had not been done before. Among other accomplishments, she'd discovered how fleas jumped, helped crack Nazi code during World War II, and produced a new kind of chicken feed from seaweed. When she was in her sixties, she had noticed modern agriculture had left fields devoid of wildflowers and arranged to have more than a thousand school fields sown with seeds from Ashton Wold, returning Chaucerian wildflowers to England.

Dame Rothschild connected Clive with the best butterfly research scientists in England and cheered the project on.

Clive thinks it may have been at his very first meeting with her that she told him the reason his butterfly exhibit was important and worth the risk was that "wonder is the beginning of philosophy"—an echo of a Socrates quote in the dialogues of Plato. It has been Clive's favorite quote and his ethos ever since. His calling, the way he sees it, is to provoke wonder.

At the butterfly house, pupae sent from around the world flourished, as did the tropical plants. The greenhouses were filled with sights that, until then, could only be seen in the jungle.

The exhibit opened in 1981, and Clive was excited, expecting that "everyone and their grandmother" would be lining up to see the marvels. But for more than a year, the exhibit had few visitors. No one knew what a butterfly house was. There simply hadn't been any before. The exhibit's financial prospects were looking grim.

Then, in 1983, Sir David Attenborough, the famous conservationist, made a series of nature documentaries that aired on the BBC. The day after an episode featuring butterflies debuted, there were lines out the London Butterfly House door.

Clive had proof of concept. He had changed the way the world thought about butterfly exhibits—taking them from lifeless shadowboxes to thriving mini-ecosystems.

Live butterfly exhibits created a larger market for butterfly breeding. In the early nineties, Clive acquired his dearest possession, the land in Belize, where he would start a butterfly farm for exporting blue morphos and other rain-forest butterflies.

When I had first contacted Clive, thinking I was just throwing out a line to someone who would never bite, he wrote back immediately—with urgency—because he wanted me to meet Ray Harberd, the founder of Belize's Fallen Stones, who was in ill health. Clive and Ray had started Fallen Stones together. It was largely Clive's money that had funded the venture, but it was Ray's ingenuity and stubborn will that had carved the breeding farm from Belizean wilderness, creating a model for protecting land and providing local jobs in a natural habitat.

Clive said Ray was the most intelligent person he had ever known. Ray was an entomologist and an adventurer who had worked for governments and oil companies. He had literally written *A Manual of Tropical Butterfly Farming*. He was an artist who painted in oils. He was tall and handsome. He could sing.

His list of attributes was so long that it was clear Ray was Clive's hero. Ray was in his nineties now, and he'd recently suffered a bad fall. Clive and I were going to visit him at his home in Wales.

On the way to Wales, Clive drove his black Mercedes fast—while making conversation and eye contact with me.

"Am I driving too fast for you?" he asked midtrip.

"No, not at all," I lied, adopting what I hoped was worldly ease while bracing in my seat. The English roads were windy and unpredictable.

I was not surprised later when I got an email from Clive mentioning he had received a speeding ticket from a hidden camera.

The Harberd home was a two-story stone house with three gables and many chimneys. Ray stood in the doorway to greet us, holding himself stiffly upright, defying age itself. He had a thick mane of bright-white hair and a full white beard.

There was a photograph on the wall inside the foyer documenting a young and strong Ray Harberd. Elsie, Ray's wife, was suffering memory loss. Clive whispered to me that she sometimes demanded to know where the young man in the photograph was and refused to believe the old man he had become was her husband. Elsie was agitated at having company, and I wasn't sure we should be there. But Ray had painstakingly prepared for our visit. In the living room, he had made stacks of chronologically arranged letters and photographs.

Clive had already told me about their life at Fallen Stones in the early days. Ray had begun the project by building a large wooden house on stilts. He and Clive each had a room in the house, with a common area in between.

There was an outside deck that stretched the length of the house.

Clive and Ray ate all their meals on the deck. For breakfast, the menu was always tropical fruit. For dinner, they alternated two meals: one night, fish curry; the next, shrimp curry. Clive remembered this time as among the happiest of his life.

"At night, I would sit there, the rain forest undulating in the distance, the glowing eyes of jungle creatures passing by below," he had told me dreamily. "And Ray and I would talk over things."

"What sort of things?" I'd asked.

"Oh," said Clive vaguely. "Whether there is a God."

Before Fallen Stones, Ray had been breeding rare butterflies in the Philippines, but guerrilla fighters had threatened his life and he'd had to leave quickly.

In Belize, he oversaw the building of the steep road to Fallen Stones. Once the road was built and the farm was up and running, Ray's family traveled from England to Belize to join him during school breaks.

The little Belizean farm grew. There was the breeding business, a small resort of rustic bungalows for adventure travelers, and even a restaurant and bar at the top of the hill.

In 2001, Ray was away on a trip to England when Hurricane Iris hit.

"It took me three days to reach Sebastian by phone," he recalled. Sebastian—the farm manager who had showed Moody and me around the butterfly pens—oversaw the day-to-day operations while Ray was away. When they finally spoke, he said, "Mr. Ray, everything is gone."

We all stared at a photograph Ray selected from a pile and laid on the carpet. It was taken when Ray returned to see the damage for himself. He was standing on the remains of some sort of deck, lumber strewn around him, one wooden chair oddly intact. He had a hand on his hip and was looking out from the top of the mountain. There was nothing. No village. No trees in the vast valley. He looked angry. Ray looked like a man who did not accept defeat easily, even from nature. On the border of the photo, he had written the number of the negative and: "Surveying the desolation Nov. 2001."

"We started to rebuild. Then came the fire," he said, his voice bitter.

Ray, I started to understand, did not remember Fallen Stones with the same hazy glow as Clive. He said it was cursed.

"But, Ray," Clive asked with a cajoling smile, "don't you ever think about the sound of the rain? The giant clouds of butterflies?"

"No," Ray said, his tone certain. "I remember hurricanes and fire. I remember the destruction of everything I built."

When we took our leave, Ray and Elsie stood in the doorway, holding hands and waving as we drove away.

From there, we sped (literally) to the Stratford Butterfly Farm.

I knew it was England's biggest butterfly farm, so I was expecting something like the San Diego Zoo or Universal Studios.

Instead, it was—while big by butterfly standards—quaint and cozy by the standard of an American tourist attraction.

We started with the public exhibit. Inside the glass enclosure, passionflower vines grew and twisted over everything. A huge iguana napped on a ledge, and beside him was a sign warning, "Watch Out.

Iguana Poo." The air was filled with fluttering butterflies, including the electric blue morphos that Fallen Stones had started exporting in the nineties.

A woman knelt down and helped her five-year-old daughter hold out her arm. A blue morpho landed on it, and when the butterfly flew away, they both giggled wildly and watched until it disappeared.

I stopped to say hello. The young mother had an Eastern European accent, and she said her visit to the exhibit brought about the first day she hadn't been thinking about being a refugee. There was magic to the place.

Clive, who was leading my tour, said butterflies tended to provoke strong reactions in people. Toddlers laughed and chased them, even if they had just been crying over an empty juice box. He said it wasn't unusual to see an adult, sitting silent and alone, letting butterflies light on them as tears slid down their face.

In a building near the exhibit, I met James, the farm manager, and Sarka, the employee who imported and exported pupae.

When Sarka entered the room, I tried to hide my surprise. I'd been expecting a ponytailed biologist in a zippered fleece. Dark-haired Sarka was wearing heels and a formfitting dress, and her eyelashes were longer than nature freely bestows. She did pole dancing classes for exercise.

James was handsome with an easy wit, traits in a young man that often make me suspicious. (Having once been a young woman and having once been susceptible to charm.) But I decided that James was not so much like Mr. Wickham—the scoundrel in Jane Austen's *Pride and Prejudice*—as the friendly neighbor who would play him in a community theater production.

There had been a time when Sarka, a multilingual Czech powerhouse, had little use for James. His easygoing ways rankled hardcharging Sarka.

But a long-ago crisis had thrown the crew of Stratford together in a fight for survival that cemented close ties.

In 2014, James had recently returned to his position as farm manager. He'd left to become a policeman because he'd felt his advancement from a butterfly-loving high-school intern to manager had hit a ceiling, and he and his wife wanted to start their family.

Still, unsure about joining a police force that was under criticism for brutality and faced with being assigned far from home, James had decided he was better off with butterflies and returned to his job. (He now had two young daughters growing up near both sets of grandparents.)

His boss, Richard, a kind-but-gruff noted entomologist, couldn't conceive of someone giving up butterflies—and to be a policeman! He had rehired James but kept him in the doghouse until the day Burt, a partner at Stratford, left on a supposed business trip but really had no intention of coming back. Burt disappeared, and so did money that kept the business running.

As checks bounced, plaintive phone calls from creditors piled up, and emails to Burt went unanswered, an unlikely team of allies rose. Because this is how the world works. When liars and cheats in power put everything—people's trust, their livelihoods, even the fate of the planet—at risk, it's up to regular people to team up and save the day. At Stratford Butterfly Farm, there was work to be done before the reclusive silent partner came to assess the damage from Burt's departure.

James took over Burt's duties. Sarka and James called their customers and suppliers. They apologized, made amends, and begged everyone to give Stratford another chance. During long, stressful days, they developed a bond as tight as siblings, including the playfulness and squabbling.

Before Burt left, he had once told Jane, a part-time gift shop worker, that if she wanted full-time work, she needed to make herself busy and indispensable. Burt had been leisurely drinking a cup of tea at the time before leaving early.

When the rumor mill had it that Burt wasn't coming back and Stratford employees began to believe the farm's days might be numbered, Jane thought, *Alright, then, time to be indispensable.*

She learned how to build a website. She checked out books from the library on advertising. She produced an eye-catching brochure that included activities for the schoolchildren who visited, which, in retrospect, seemed like it shouldn't have been a novel idea.

Pink-cheeked Jane with her graying ponytail and love of fuzzy cardigans made herself into the marketing director and would increase the number of visitors by nearly forty thousand in five years.

Richard, Jane, James, and Sarka believed that if they had things running smoothly when the now sole owner did show up, he wouldn't shut them down.

Six months after Burt disappeared, that sole owner, Clive Farrell, left his estate in Dorset and arrived at Stratford to sort out the losses. He had supplied the funds to build the exhibit in 1985 and then handed over the day-to-day operations to Burt so he could concentrate on other business ventures and his gardens and butterflies in Dorset.

Burt's betrayal had gutted him. Clive had considered Burt a close friend. He was left wondering how he could ever trust anyone again.

But when he arrived in Stratford and saw what the determined crew had accomplished, he also saw that they were capable of running the business. As he worked alongside them to untangle the books, Clive was drawn into a growing sense of kinship at Stratford.

He soon found his fear of not being able to trust anyone disappearing. He trusted, maybe even loved, this small crew who had scrambled and defied the odds.

By protecting the Stratford Butterfly Farm, the English crew had also protected Fallen Stones and the crew in Belize. They had helped support more than a dozen families in a Mayan village and safeguarded a swath of Belizean rain forest.

Coworkers who had never met depended upon one another. Ray Harberd's photograph of total devastation from the hurricane was fresh in my mind. Clive's butterfly empire was precarious, precious, and totally dependent on a group of devoted individuals battling any number of threats, all of whom shared an intertwined fate with butterflies.

Shortly after I was introduced to James and Sarka, word came that the box from Belize had arrived. All formalities came to a halt. In another room, James and Sarka quickly started unpacking pupae from boxes like the ones I'd seen Sebastian and his team pack up on our trip to Fallen Stones. Each chrysalis was nestled in a hollow of foam rubber. They each had to be wiggled out gently because they could crush easily. Then the pupae had to be sorted, counted, repacked, and sent on their web of journeys.

I asked if I could help, and they let me. As I worked, I could picture the workers at Fallen Stones putting the box together.

James and Sarka would soon be able to picture the connection for themselves. They told me, with no small amount of excitement, that they were going to attend a butterfly conference in Florida. Afterward, they would travel on to Belize and see—for the first time—the place where their pupae came from. They would finally meet their Fallen Stones counterparts.

Of course, I asked if I could tag along.

Four

FLORIDA

In November 2019, the International Association of Butterfly Exhibitors and Suppliers (IABES) met in Orlando, Florida. Some of the topics—"Using Emergence and Longevity Data to Optimize Pupae"— sounded over my head. But organizers also promised outings to "rival the 1998 trip to Butterfly Dan's in Kissimmee." (Who could forget?)

The Florida trip was my starting gun. After England, I had returned to my reporting job and our home in California. But now I was going to take a year off to write about a butterfly farm. (Newspapers are prepared for their employees to wander off on various projects.)

I met James and Sarka in the lobby of the hotel where the butterfly conference was being held. Sarka was wearing a reptile-print dress, heels, and she'd dyed her hair a magenta red. (She never kept any one color too long, she told me.) James was at the front desk trying, unsuccessfully, to flirt his way to a room upgrade.

At that night's icebreaker, in one of the conference hotel's ballrooms, I first met the "butterfly people," as they tended to call themselves. Some, like Susan from Saratoga Springs, were hobbyists who bred local butterflies. Susan took her butterflies to memory care centers. The idea started when her mother's Alzheimer's progressed until she had no memory of Susan's deceased father, the man she'd been married to for sixty years. People who could recall very little often remembered Susan when she visited the centers with her fine mesh cages full of butterflies. She attributed the phenomenon to an intrinsic human connection to beauty that, she insisted, reaches deeper than individual memory.

Others, like Rich, were cornerstones of a commercial industry. Rich's business was the main nucleus for butterfly delivery in North America. James and Sarka had him pegged as their biggest competitor. I could tell he was a big shot with the butterfly crowd because people were circling for an audience with him. But his attention was focused on telling me about his newest venture: fireflies.

He explained that they're difficult to breed because many firefly species are carnivorous and will, if given the opportunity, eat one another. He needed to find a breed that preferred vegetation. It also had to be a species that flies around. The ones who just sit there blinking might as well be LED lights. He was working on breeding some flitty fireflies from Taiwan that are gregarious—which, in a scientific context, means they don't eat their own kind.

There were a hundred attendees at the conference from all over the world, especially places where there are exotic butterflies such as Costa Rica, the Philippines, Thailand, India, and Kenya. A breeding farm could be run by a family who specialized in one butterfly or a well-staffed operation like Fallen Stones in Belize that produced a quarter of the butterflies in the atrium at Stratford and supplied orders from other exhibitors, as well. Some exhibitors came from small museums in towns like Sioux Falls, South Dakota, or they helped run massive zoos, like the one in the center of Rotterdam in the Netherlands that saw 1.6 million visitors a year. I noticed Walt Disney World had sent a representative.

The only attendee who reminded me of how I had previously imagined a butterfly person looking was seventy-nine-year-old Gareth, who I could easily imagine in a pith helmet, wielding a butterfly net.

Bearded, bespectacled Gareth was from a mining village in North England, and his words rolled with a thick burr. He wasn't sporting a helmet, but each day, he wore the same outfit: a safari vest with pins of a remembrance poppy and a blue morpho. He always had his camera around his neck, and the leather strap was engraved with his name.

He was missing a front tooth. Gareth told me this was because he'd made a practical choice. He met the same friends at his local pub every week, and he was at the age when there were more and more empty chairs. When he fell off a ladder and knocked out his tooth, he'd decided he might not have enough years left to get his money's worth out of dentistry.

I sat next to Gareth on the two-hour bus ride to the Florida Museum of Natural History at the University of Florida for a conference field trip. He had missed the previous conference because he was foraging in Borneo—or was it the Philippines?—he couldn't recall. He told me about rowing down the Amazon, chasing butterflies in Cameroon, and the time he'd built football stadiums for Gaddafi in exchange for a chance to build a butterfly house in Tripoli. He'd ended up helping England navigate that dictator. I discreetly looked up his last claim on my phone and was greeted with a newspaper article accompanied by a photo of a young Gareth wearing a tailored suit, all teeth present.

We were sitting directly behind the bus driver, a large man with a deep voice who was singing to Keith Sweat's "I Want to Love You Down." The driver was dancing in his seat, drumming on the console. Some butterfly people shyly semi-swayed.

Next, an Aretha Franklin classic came on, and Gareth danced in his seat to "R-E-S-P-E-C-T" emboldening the others. He told me there was a time when he had fancied discos.

At the museum, we toured the McGuire Center for Lepidoptera, which had one of the largest collections of butterflies in the world with more than ten million specimens. Many had been donated by surviving family members of butterfly collectors. The center kept the specimens in drawers as if they were library catalog cards.

Before there was a live butterfly industry, there was a secretive butterfly trade. Wealthy collectors paid great amounts to pin a dead exotic butterfly in a book. Actually, strike the "before." There is still a black market for dead endangered butterflies. But this was a trade show for a live counterforce—a global butterfly industry that had not existed until the eighties, after Clive turned his childhood passion into an audience draw. Clive's London Butterfly House had been replicated all over the world, including by Clive, who had some successes and some spectacular failures in various locations. The exhibits these butterfly enthusiasts and lepidopterists built created a demand for pupae, which created jobs in the rain forest and other places that did not involve logging or other industry that harmed the environment. Their work helped preserve native habitats all over the world, because to breed butterflies, you needed butterfly host and feeding plants. The butterflies in captivity protected the land for wild butterflies and other creatures.

What I had previously thought of as a band of quirky enthusiasts was a consequential part of the environmentalist movement.

The conference finale was a trip to Butterfly Dan's, owned by Dan, who traced his interest in butterflies to his first-grade teacher bringing a milkweed plant to school that attracted a monarch. Butterfly Dan's was the biggest breeder of Florida butterflies, and one of their clients was Butterfly World, the first US butterfly exhibit. It had opened in Coconut Creek, Florida, in 1988 and Clive was a partner.

Sarka was my seatmate on the tour bus. Our conversation turned to her childhood. She was left at age two, she told me, in a violent home. The creature she had been closest to was her German shepherd, Eros. She was there for Eros when the dog suffered abuse, and he was there for Sarka when she was the one hurt.

Sarka had a luminous smile, a seventeen-year marriage, and a job she was passionate about that revolved around fragile, resilient creatures.

She confidently told me that she was happy in life. Someone who had been trapped in violence for her first fifteen years of life had found her way to something so much better.

When she asked me why I wanted to write about butterflies, my first thought was that I liked stories about miracles—and that she'd just told me one. Everything I'd learned about the butterfly farm had that similar quality to it: the ability to thrive despite circumstance and odds. But aloud, I said that I had witnessed and written about a terrible California drought. The desperate families, dying wildlife, and raging wildfires had left me hyperaware of looming environmental collapse. Butterflies were some of the most vulnerable organisms to climate change, and I was drawn to stories about protecting them.

I didn't get into this next part, but I felt as if the environmental threat had seeped into my very cells over the years of drought and fires. Yet life went on. I continued to fret about split ends and sentence structure. I could get a bit frantic about having fun. (While there was still time!) I didn't know how to fit it all together—the existential threat and the daily delights.

I didn't even get to consider myself unique. So many people were reporting this same feeling of disconnection that psychologists had been coming up with names for it: "eco-anxiety," "climate grief."

In some ways, that disconnection was a familiar feeling. My parents had died when I was a teenager, and for a long time, I had taken living in the moment to the extreme. Sit in class for an important test that I had studied for? Not if it was a perfect beach day. After all, I reminded myself more often than was perhaps healthy: we're all going to die. For most of my youth, I had been a pro at carpe diem who had lost her ability to imagine a future.

This climate anxiety, now, was a mirror of my personal grief on a global scale. But, why butterflies?

They are both ephemeral and eternal. Through time, across cultures, they have been symbols of hope, rebirth, resurrection, transitions, the human soul.

A 2018 study of fossils shows that butterflies and moths have been on Earth about two hundred million years, pushing their origins back some seventy million years than earlier believed. They're older than flowers. They survived a mass extinction of life prior to the Jurassic Period.

In today's environment, butterflies are the celebratory confetti tossed in the air when the plants and air and water and the rest of the insect world are healthy. If you get it right for butterflies, you have it right for the rest of the ecosystem.

Like everything else, they are under threat. The decreasing number of butterfly species is alarming. Some 60 percent of those left are dependent on rain forest, an environment that is also rapidly disappearing. But, for now, despite everything, butterflies exist.

If you happened to be a person trying to appreciate the beauty of everyday moments and the wonder of nature while also believing that we are marching toward the end of the world, there might be worse ideas than spending time on a rain-forest-conserving butterfly farm next to the ruins of a fallen civilization.

At Butterfly Dan's, we divided into two groups. The first group boarded the Bug Tram for a tour of the butterfly-feeding plants of southern Florida. The rest of us were left to socialize and, in my case, recall that I had a dormant phobia.

It might not seem like the sort of thing one would forget. But I didn't come across too many snakes in my regular life. At this time, I didn't even think of it as a phobia. I would have just told you I had a "thing" about snakes. Like when I was watching the original *Jungle Book* movie as an adult and screamed when the singing cartoon snake came down the tree. I don't like heights, but I once rappelled down a towering boulder rather than pass a rattlesnake slumbering on the trail.

The rest of my hiking group walked around the fat, coiled sunbather without incident.

During the butterfly convention, snakes—as well as poisonous plants, bugs, frogs, and insects that lay eggs under your skin—were frequent cocktail conversation. The attendees were people who crawled around the jungle finding all of the world's creatures fascinating—and the poisonous ones were particularly exciting to this crew.

Their voices dropped and their storytelling grew dramatic when they described sightings of a fer-de-lance, a snake that isn't just highly venomous but aggressive. It will even give chase to a human.

I got a prickly feeling on my skin and exited whenever I sensed a snake anecdote in the offing.

But on that day, stranded outside a bus and waiting for my turn at the tour, I didn't have time to dodge. A man who kept calling Zimbabwe by the colonial name of Rhodesia and talking over his young Belizean assistant, Elias, grabbed me by the arm and pulled me into a circle of people, where he was proudly showing a video.

"You must see this gorgeous creature we recently freed in Belize," he said.

In the video, several men set down a large white bag. The bag opened from the inside, and a boa constrictor slowly unwound itself out of the bag. It kept coming and coming—a seven-foot snake emerged. Little stars floated in front of my eyes. I stepped back. The man's response to my recoiling was to grab my arm and hold his phone closer to my face.

"You must watch. He's a magnificent creature. Absolutely beautiful," he insisted. I threw off his arm more forcefully than could be considered polite and left the circle, gulping air while the boa continued to draw admiring exclamations.

Elias, the watchful assistant, noticed me hyperventilating and brought me a cup of water.

"I'm sorry," I told him. "It's embarrassing. But I think I have a snake phobia."

"I understand," he said. "I have a wasp phobia."

"Wasps?" I asked. "Were you always afraid of them?"

"I was respectful," he said. "In Belize, we grow up knowing there is a wasp's sting that can paralyze a person."

A few years earlier, he had been stung. He'd felt something on his neck. Before he could slap it away, he'd felt searing pain. He awoke in the hospital paralyzed, his entire body swollen. His survival had been touch-and-go for five days.

"Now, it is a phobia," he said. "If someone says 'wasp,' my head starts pounding."

"I think to be a phobia, it has to be an unreasonable fear," I told him. "That is entirely reasonable." His kindness had distracted me, and soon we were ready for our turn riding the tram through gardens and flight houses.

Come evening, Butterfly Dan's transformed for a low-country boil. Awnings went up, tables came out, and steaming buckets of seasoned sausage, shrimp, crab, potatoes, and corn were dumped on plastic-covered tables to be devoured with communal delight.

Burning torches cast everything in a rich amber glow and filled the air with smoke that did little to discourage the swarms of mosquitoes. The mood was both festive and pensive as people lined up for ice cream made with dry ice, and said their goodbyes.

Later that night, back at the hotel, I tried to count my bites as I dabbed on Benadryl but kept losing track in the upper teens. Michael Mayhew of Martian Taco fame happened to text at that moment.

I gave him a quick rundown that I was in Florida after a low-country boil and leaving for Belize the next day, which turned out to not be a good idea because I was very afraid of snakes and it was home to a particularly nasty looking seven-footer.

After first giving me several restaurant recommendations where I could eat more boiled corn and potatoes, MM latched upon my phobia.

He is a documentary editor with a film degree, so he thought my nausea and aversion were excellent news for my story:

GRAY TEXT BUBBLE: This type of narrative follows classic story structure: Character has a goal (jungle), Character has a really hard obstacle (snakes), Character struggles to overcome obstacle (gets help). For people with PTSD there is a special, very specific type of therapy that helps to gradually make them comfortable with the sights or sounds that trigger them. You could do the same type of therapy for snakes. That could be a very funny chapter!

BLUE TEXT BUBBLE: What is funny is that you think I should habituate to SNAKES. I hate you.

Five

THE JUNGLE HOUSE

The nine-seat Cessna that would fly James, Sarka, and me on our last leg from Belize City to PG waited on an empty, rainy tarmac.

Sarka has promised to hold James's hand. I wished I was in on the deal. I was with James: "What's wrong with driving?"

But once in the air, the view won me over: white beaches, deep-green mangroves, a turquoise sea stamped with cloud shadows. James distracted himself by chatting with the passenger in front of him—a health-care worker on her way to an outbreak of dengue fever. Sarka shot video and took photos with the thoroughness of a one-woman documentary crew.

The terminal where we landed, a tan one-room building with a lopsided awning and a sun-bleached sign, sat in the shade of a mango tree.

Clive had arrived the day before and was waiting to greet us. I was happy to see him. I was also happy to see that Eduardo was driving.

Things had changed with Eduardo and Alli since I'd last seen them. He had received an unsolicited job offer that promised the family more financial security. Now he was in charge of safety for a company that had manufacturing plants around the world. He had taken the job even though it meant being based in Kansas City, Missouri. Like us, he was visiting Belize.

Alli said she could never go back. She had fallen in love with jungle life. She was running the hotel and acting as business manager for the butterfly farm. The boys were enrolled in a local Belizean school.

Clive told me he'd asked Alli if she and Eduardo were getting a divorce. To his great relief, she had laughed. She said it wasn't like that.

I wondered what it was like, but I didn't know her well enough to ask.

That night, we all had dinner together at a restaurant with a deck that stretched out over the sea and box cheese graters over light bulbs for ambiance. Eduardo complimented Alli's beauty and intelligence several times.

I said to Alli, out of earshot of Eduardo, "He's such a romantic. So many compliments."

Alli, a Midwest native who'd met Eduardo when they were both grad students in Australia, rolled her eyes.

"He's always like that. He's from Colombia."

Across the table, another conversation caught my attention. Clive was telling Sarka and James how delighted he was that Moody and I would be living in "Clive's House" when I returned for my longer reporting trip.

"I do believe the house has been lonely," he said.

Clive had offered us the house where he and Ray had lived decades ago. I had told him I was grateful for the option. But I didn't consider it a done deal. I was still hoping to find some miraculous steal on a beach rental where I could convince my friends to visit me. One with a warm shower.

As far as I knew, no one had lived in Clive's House for thirty years. If we stayed there, we would be alone in the jungle after the workers left for the day, and I had listened carefully when Clive described the glowing eyes of animals at night.

I had tried to express my appreciation of the gracious offer, but what had I said that made him think I had accepted? I started feeling anxious.

Early the next morning, David, a butterfly farm employee, picked the four of us up at Hickatee for the trip to Fallen Stones, driving Eduardo's truck. David was from San Pedro Columbia, as were all the workers at the butterfly farm. He was single-handedly running a new breeding center on land next to Hickatee to provide Stratford with butterflies who preferred lower elevations. When David smiled, everyone else did too, like when one person yawns and everyone else in the room gets sleepy. I liked him immediately.

It was the rainy season, so the road's potholes were now ponds. David had to gun the engine and try to keep the tires on the thin ridges of mud sticking out of the water.

Sebastian greeted our group at the top, the same as when Moody and I had visited, but this time, the view was shrouded in clouds. It rained as we picked our way down the wet, slick rocks.

"Sebastian, you said it wasn't going to rain," Clive said.

"It isn't raining, Mr. Clive. It is sprinkling," Sebastian said.

My first glimpse of the house—from outside and at a distance—surprised me. It was large, made of beautiful wood, high up on stilts, with a balcony stretching the entire length. The fact that it stood was a miracle. We had passed several stone foundations where structures used to stand before the hurricane.

The kitchen was a separate building below the house. I was behind Sebastian when he opened the door, and I saw over his shoulder bugs scattering into the darkness.

"I must tell them that the kitchen is not open," Sebastian said, his face serious.

There was a concrete counter, a sink, and what looked like an oversized trivet, but it could be hooked up to propane and become a cooking range.

Clive poked his head in.

"Sebastian, good news. Diana and her partner, Moody, may stay here. We must get them a propane refrigerator. That's what's needed!"

I was cheered to hear the word "may." But he then added, "Isn't it wonderful? I do believe the house has been lonely."

The house wasn't that lonely. More than a dozen bats were Velcroed to the wall next to the stairwell.

"Oh, look," Sarka cooed. "Aren't they cute?"

They were not cute. They had rodent ears, mini pig snouts, and vampire wings. They were furry, not like a dog but like mold on peaches.

We opened the door to the house. A bat swooped out. I did not scream. I was probably the only one in the group who had to work at that.

Inside, it was dim, but there was enough light to see the beds were stacked high with the foam Sebastian's crew used to pack butterfly boxes. I wondered what lived inside the mattresses beneath the towers of foam rubber.

Oil paints that had belonged to Ray Harberd were still sitting on a table by one of the bedroom's windows. Some tubes were squeezed and opened. They were dried solid with yellowing labels. I sent thoughts to Wales and hoped Ray had once painted clouds of butterflies.

Using my phone's flashlight, I looked around the dark bathroom. There was a stained sink and a cinder-block shower. I eyed the drain and wondered what might crawl out.

Sarka's voice floated over from the bathroom in the other room.

"There's a scorpion in the shower," she called out, delighted with her find.

James and Sarka went on to find a midsize tarantula and a Jesus Christ lizard. James told me the common name of the *Basiliscus basiliscus* lizard is because they run on water or alternatively because people say "Jesus Christ!" when one darts across their foot.

James and Sarka leaned on the rail of the balcony enthusing over the house's splendors.

"I would love to live here in the middle of the rain forest. Who wouldn't?" Sarka asked.

"It's spectacular," said James. "Why, if someone wanted ocean and beaches, they could go to Greece or whatnot. Whereas this is *real* rain forest."

I would describe them as staring off into the undulating jungle, except the forest had crept in and enveloped the house, so visibility was about three feet.

There is a video that I made for Moody so he could see the house for himself. I narrated it in what I felt was a strictly observational tone: "Here is the room. It has windows. It also has bats. Here is the rain forest. It comes right up to the house." Listening to it now, I must concede a faint note of hysteria. I do not sound like someone who would consider a Greek isle a bore.

We next toured the farm. Having been there before, I felt very in the know. James and Sarka complimented the workers at each butterfly house and asked detailed questions about how many leaves each sort of butterfly ate and how long they pupated and what time of year there were the most eggs.

The employee at the last house had clearly prepared for Clive's visit. His hair was freshly cut and combed to the side with precision. He appeared nervous.

Sebastian introduced him as Manuel Cal, but I would come to know him as Sammy, and I would never again see his hair parted or him standing so still. Sammy was far more likely to be found climbing a banana tree or gesturing as much as, well, me, when he talked.

Sebastian told Clive that this young man was breeding an *Aeria eurimedia* butterfly.

"Fantastic," breathed Clive, who had always wanted this particular butterfly, as Sebastian knew.

Sammy began to tell the story of his discovery, shyly dipping his head and barely able to make eye contact, but soon, he was gathering speed and recounting the day as if reliving it.

One day, outside the hut where he spent hours feeding caterpillars, he noticed a wild butterfly. It was zebra-striped in pale greenish yellow and black, with a coral stripe on each end of the wings and a border of black with white polka dots. When he'd asked Sebastian about the butterfly, Sebastian had told him it was an *Aeria eurimedia* and that Clive longed to have it.

"After that, his eyes are wide open, and he is always looking around with his butterfly net," Sebastian said.

Sammy was determined to breed a butterfly that Fallen Stones had never exported. His goal in life was to dazzle the whole butterfly world with his discoveries, and the first step to that was getting Clive's recognition with this butterfly. One day on his lunch break, Sammy netted one of the *Aeria eurimedia* just outside the shack where he works.

He reenacted the moment so convincingly that we all turned and looked as if it were still happening right there outside the hut.

He had caught the butterfly flitting in midair. Because of the timing, he didn't know its host plant. He hadn't actually witnessed the butterfly feeding or laying eggs.

"*Prestonia,*" said Clive, who I believe knows every word written about every butterfly.

"Yes, Mr. Clive," Sebastian said. "But we must find the *Prestonia* that this butterfly likes."

Flower and butterfly evolutions are so entwined that there is often one particular subspecies of butterfly that will only lay eggs on one particular subspecies of a plant.

Clive wondered if a similar subspecies would suffice. But Manuel and Sebastian had found it would not. None of the types of *Prestonia*, a flowering plant with a milky sap, that they had tried worked. This was one picky butterfly. They'd had to let that first butterfly go before it starved in captivity.

"But I said to myself, 'I will keep looking,'" Sammy told us, continuing the story.

One day in San Antonio, a Mopan Maya village to the west, Sammy spotted the butterfly and "followed and followed and followed" through plants along the riverbank, and then it happened. He saw the butterfly turn and put her eggs on the underside of a leaf.

"I went, *whoa!*" Sammy said.

"Fantastic!" said Clive.

The butterfly had led him to the host plant. Sammy dug up the plant with the eggs and took it to Fallen Stones.

Now he and Sebastian were trying to propagate the plant for caterpillars.

They already had three hundred lush green plants growing, but they needed more. Sammy now had seventy butterflies that were about to lay eggs. They came from the first eggs he'd harvested in San Antonio.

Clive looked delighted. Sammy again ducked his head, but this time, he was smiling. We all looked to a flight cage where the striped butterflies floated around colorful flowers. Sammy and Sebastian seemed to watch with the same awe as our group of visitors, who were seeing it for the first time.

From the house, we hiked to a waterfall on the edge of Clive's property. Before, when Sebastian had said it was sprinkling, I would have held that it was raining.

During the hike, it was truly coming down, and I saw his point. The canopy was so thick that we were remarkably dry, but the rain pounded the leaves overhead with a thundering beat.

My eyes were darting around like those of George, our hypervigilant herding-breed dog. I knew that snakes hung out in trees as well as slithered on the ground in this jungle. I seemed to be the only one with concerns.

The downpour grew even harder, penetrating the canopy, and I couldn't see because of the river washing over my face.

"We're going to have to find shelter," Sebastian shouted, which merely perplexed me, because: Where? All that surrounded us were trees and green, and excellent hiding places for all types of unknown animals.

He herded us all beneath a slender palm. I didn't like being off-trail. He darted into the forest.

One at a time, he brought us "Mayan umbrellas"—poster-board-size palm fronds. Thus equipped, we carried on down the trail, fronds over our heads, like a parade of sodden surreys with the fringe on top.

I once hiked a chunk of the John Muir Trail in the Sierra Nevada, managing to fall into several rivers. So when we came to a stream, I was already aware that balancing on wet rocks is not one of my fortes. It's always that first jump from bank to river that feels most treacherous.

James put down his palm frond and offered me a hand. I hesitated. Earlier, Sarka had told me a story about breaking up a dog fight. Her dog, a Staffordshire terrier that she loves dearly, once got in a fight with a dog of the same strong-jawed breed. Sarka reached between them, got her wrist broken, and drove herself to the hospital.

You didn't want to act dainty in front of someone as fearless as Sarka. On the other hand, I didn't want to fall in the stream. I took James's hand, hoping Sarka wasn't looking.

The waterfall was three flat pools that gently dropped one into the other. Ferns and fronds feathered the banks. The beauty of the spot should have dazzled me, but it seemed overly familiar. I'm from Palm Springs. This was replicated in the lobby of many a Marriott. I wondered if I was missing out on the calm feeling that nature usually gave me because, to me, dripping green jungle was standard desert-resort artifice.

The return hike was a steep slog. I slipped once and wore a stripe of mud on my pants and face. Clive and I were bringing up the rear, so we had a chance to talk. I had met his wife, Rajna, a beautiful Serbian poet, and knew she had little interest in Fallen Stones. Her tastes were more cosmopolitan. I was curious to know about his two adult children. I wondered if either of them was interested in carrying on his work with butterflies.

They had other interests, Clive explained. His daughter "made the best cat collars in all of London," according to Clive. If I wanted one, Clive could get me a 15 percent discount. His son wanted to start a business exporting hand-hammered *kadai*, an Indian cooking pot shaped like a wok but with steeper sides.

Clive had brought his son on a trip to Fallen Stones when he was about ten years old. They had been hiking in the jungle with guides in front. There was a fer-de-lance on the trail. It raised up from a coil and waved its head. One of the guides crouched down and shot it between its eyes.

"That made me sad," Clive said. "It was a beautiful creature. But they can be quite dangerous."

His son, Luke, now in his thirties, still vividly remembered that trip. From a ten-year-old boy's perspective, it had been a great adventure. It didn't sound so appealing to me.

It was late afternoon when we reached the top of the hill and waited for David to pick us up. We hadn't eaten since breakfast. Clive picked a handful of wild lemongrass for me to smell. It was all I could do to not grab it and stuff it in my mouth.

At Hickatee, we went our separate ways to rest and clean up. On the way to my room, I was surprised to come across Alli sitting on a bench. Alli, I'd observed, was in constant motion. Her idea of free time was painting a bathroom. But her lounging that afternoon was purposeful. She was trying out some furniture she'd had a local carpenter carve for the grounds. I joined her for consumer testing, taking a seat on the smooth wood beneath the thatched roof of the bicycle stand.

I told Alli I had a stomachache over needing to tell Clive I didn't want to stay in his house. I was also tense because I still had not found any other house for rent near the farm. Now that I had the lay of the land, I could see any beach-house idea wouldn't work. It was too far of a drive from the butterfly farm. Especially with that final hill. But there must be something in the area? Alli couldn't think of a single lead. The only town nearby was the Mayan village where families shared land and built another house when their offspring were married. It wasn't the custom to rent. She said that even if I managed to find something there, Clive's House would be less rustic.

I thought to myself that even if I was a Rothschild-type heiress who could afford a long-term stay at Hickatee with my tea being delivered in the mornings, it would put me forty-five minutes from the farm on a road that was not supposed to be driven at night.

I kept the stomachache even as I realized I wasn't going to have to talk to Clive about not accepting the offer. I was going to tell him, "Thank you very much. We look forward to keeping the house company."

"Alli," I said. "How do you do it? The bugs and the snakes and the heat and the rain? I feel on edge all the time. I think things are biting me even when they aren't."

"Do you really want to know my secret?" she asked.

I nodded.

"Gin," she said. "Every night. Sometimes in the afternoon too."

I laughed.

"I'm not joking," she said, her eyes big. "I love it here. But it can get hard."

Two days later, James, Sarka, and I returned to Miami (from there, James and Sarka would travel on to England—if they ever made it through the immigration line that had Sarka fuming). Clive was leaving later in the week. To save room in my suitcase, I flew in my clunky trail boots and permanently mud-stained trousers. I had scheduled a lay-over so I could visit my friend Jordan, who had been in the fellowship program with me.

The car pulled up to a huge glass tower of a building with an infinity pool in front of the valet parking. Jordan came down wearing a long-sleeved black blouse, dressy black shorts, and taupe platform sandals. Her long blond hair was loose, and her always-golden tan was deeper. I was seeing Jordan in her natural habitat, far from Harvard Yard.

We walked into a lobby of floor-to-ceiling windows and artwork by names I might have recognized had I spent more time strolling high-end galleries. A security guard scurried over. Jordan said I was her guest, but the woman looked at my boots that were dropping bits of now-dried jungle mud on the gleaming floors and asked to see two forms of ID.

Jordan's twenty-seventh-floor condo had white marble floors and a glass wall with a view of Biscayne Bay. After a shower, I put on white sweatpants and a white tank top, feeling I should try to not clash with the decor.

Jordan had just returned from Europe and the funeral of a dear friend. She wanted to talk about anything else for a bit.

I told her about Clive's House. I thought it would give her a laugh to hear how ridiculously prissy I was being over a few bats and it would give me comfort to hear my fears mocked.

But when I finished, she said, "Good God."

She asked if I had photos. I did, and a video. She expanded the photo of the shower floor.

She said, "Good God. Fuck."

I was alarmed because this was not what I'd expected of Jordan: She had spent her career in war zones. She had run a news network's coverage out of Kabul, living in places so vile that she'd chosen to sleep outside and take her chances with snipers.

She looked at the photos of the trail to the waterfall.

"Marcum," she said, lowering her voice. "Do you know where they send British special forces for a make-it-or-break-it test?" Not waiting for me to answer, she said, "The jungles of Belize."

Jordan said she had been friends with a man who had trained in every sort of environment, and then the jungle broke him. It left him sitting in a tree, trembling, unable to move.

I had to let that sink in for a second: the forest that the butterfly people love and trek through gathering caterpillar food is the same jungle that breaks men trained in guerrilla warfare. One culture's idea of untold dangers was another's nature walk.

I cast about for a positive side.

"There are so many butterfly species there," I said. "Belize is one of the most biodiverse places on Earth."

"Exactly," said Jordan. "The jungle is teeming with every kind of creature, most of them predators that want to eat you, be it mosquitoes or jaguars." I decided that Jordan was not the person to go to for reassurance.

When I got back home to Fresno, I walked in our front door and, still holding my suitcase, told Moody that the house had bats and that Clive had once gone for an evening walk and, the next day, the workers had found jaguar prints following his. And, also, British special forces freaked out in the jungle.

"Awesome!" said Moody, with genuine delight. "I have always wanted to see a jaguar."

Six

TSUNAMIS AND SPIDERS

Moody and I waited until after hurricane season to head south. We started by driving north from California to Oregon to leave the dogs on their own extended vacation with our friends Joe and Donna and their Bernese mountain dog, Willie. While we were away, Murphy and George would go to the beach and frolic on sand dunes. They would miss out on *real* rain forest. But they would not be eaten by jaguars.

Clive had proven to be a wonderful pen pal. He wrote letters full of travels and butterflies and, recently, updates on the house.

Along the way, I read Moody bits from the latest:

"I have authorized Alli to acquire the fridge, solar panel, and get the house right for your move. I think you will get to love the bats, they are such beautiful creatures and I can safely say they are not the vampire type!"

Joe and Moody had been best friends since high school. In their twenties, they had spent almost two years traveling the world together. The morning of our flight, I was sitting on Joe and Donna's deck with a mug of coffee, breathing in the cool ocean air. Moody was showing Joe photos of Belize.

Joe said, "Hey, Jack, remember on our trip, that time in southern India?"

Another traveler had tipped them off about a wilderness area where there were Bengal tigers and visitors could sleep on raised platforms while the tigers roamed below.

When they'd arrived at the protected area, there were no other people and one trail leading into the jungle. "Early in the going, we spotted a very long snake," Joe said. "Spying us, it raised up and flared out its hood. I realized it was a cobra. So, I'm thinking, *Okay, let's back off,* and what does this fricking guy do?" he asked, jerking his head to Moody. "He walks toward the thing. The snake backs up. Jack walks closer."

"I'd never seen a cobra," Moody said.

Joe and I glared at him.

"I was twenty," he said.

The cobra went down a hole that was behind him. The story didn't end there. Joe and Moody walked on, Joe told me, coming to a deeply wooded area.

"Big broadleaf trees. A huge canopy. It was like entering a tunnel," Joe said. "We hadn't gone fifty yards when the whole place erupted in monkey screams. It was a monkey cacophony, loud and unsettling."

They considered whether they should turn back, but not very seriously. The woods soon gave way to towering grass.

"I thought, *Oh! That's what elephant grass is—grass so tall it could obscure an elephant,*" Joe said. "Then, all of a sudden came the blast of a wild elephant. It was so loud and present, like right inside me. Without even thinking, I climbed a tree, shimmied right up. I saw two elephants, and one was a little one."

"Did Moody climb a tree?" I asked.

"No," said Moody. "I was trying to hear if there was a pissed-off bull elephant and what direction. And, Joe—you weren't very far up that tree. And there was only one tree. And you were in it."

They didn't spend the night on any platform.

"We talked it over and decided it might be best to get the hell out of there," Joe said.

The points I took from the story were that Moody had walked toward a cobra, ignored monkey warnings, stayed on the ground near a protective elephant mother, and then needed to talk over whether it was best to not stay and sleep there.

I was quiet as we packed up.

"What's wrong?" Moody asked.

"I'm afraid you're going to get us killed," I said.

"Oh, that. Don't worry," said Moody. "Everything will be fine."

Always a terrifying sentence.

Actually, I, too, had mostly entered the "everything will be fine" stage.

There are, in my experience, three stages to getting ready for a journey.

Stage One:
CONSIDER EVERYTHING THAT CAN GO WRONG.

For example, on our trip to Belize, there could be bat rabies, snakebites, wasp-sting paralysis, and/or discomfort brought on by rustic quarters and no access to hot water.

To make the most of this stage, you should throw in some personal inadequacies:

"I am *no* Indiana Jones, other than a shared repulsion of snakes."

"My hair will be a Brillo pad in that humidity."

"Moody doesn't listen to monkeys when they're clearly trying to tell him something."

Stage One is a time to get expansive with imagined calamities: drug cartels, off-season hurricanes, army ants. If you're in need of ideas, be sure and visit online travel forums. Don't limit the imagination. Think big!

Stage Two:
SMUGLY FOIL POSSIBLE CALAMITY WITH THE PERFECT PACKING LIST.

Whatever you're facing, all it takes is careful planning, you tell yourself.

For example, the jungle house was rustic. No problem. We would want to leave the house improved to thank Clive, and if you're buying for the house of a millionaire, you should splurge, right?

So, linen sheets. Perfect white linen sheets on the beds. Sage-colored summer-weight quilts for the foot of the beds. Dining plates in cream and bowls in bright olive. Bye-bye dreary, hello jungle chic.

"There is no place that can't be transformed with the proper textiles" is a motto that I cling to during Stage Two.

With smug self-satisfaction, I checked off a legal pad's worth of lists and shipped the house and kitchen items off to Belize almost three months before our arrival.

In my suitcase, I would bring knee-high rubber boots (take that, snakes and hurricanes) and anti-frizz hair potion.

As for things like cartels and highly organized ants, at Stage Two, a person is too busy packing to think about these more abstract worries and has already dwarfed those thoughts by naming them in Stage One.

Stage Three:
EVERYTHING WILL BE ALRIGHT.

Once you are moving on down the highway, got the radio on, and your feet on the dashboard (please refer to variety of country and/or rock songs for further imagery), the first two stages become ancient history. One way or the other, you are on your way and will deal with whatever you do or don't have when you get there.

I'll use our trip as an example. We were on the road trip to Oregon when I got an email from Alli telling me the shipment had still not arrived (eleven weeks after being mailed) and might be delayed another month. She would try to go to the mercantile and outfit the house. Even two days before, I had been mentally reviewing the contents in that box. I was certain everything it contained was essential and transformative. Now there was no box, but I had feet on dashboard/wind in hair/favorite song on radio, and my reaction was: "Whatever. Everything will be fine."

Did not climbers sleep in little hammocks on the side of El Capitan? Had I not once thrown a dinner party for thirty dollars? Things can always be accomplished with less than you would imagine.

In Belize, we rented a Jeep and drove from Belize City to Toledo. Our last stop before Fallen Stones was in PG for groceries.

I was eyeing Perrier water, wondering if it would be useless considering my plan to drink a lot of gin and tonics, when something caught my attention. Usually, I am an eavesdropper extraordinaire. I don't consider it rude—I consider it my writer superpower. But it took me a little while to tune into the conversation at the checkout line. I'm not sure how many times I heard the word "tsunami" before it registered in my brain.

Making my way to the front of the store, I looked up at the television that was suspended from the ceiling. The crawl on the screen said: "Tsunami Advisory Warning following 7.7 earthquake in Jamaica. Seek higher ground."

"Excuse me," I asked the small group at the counter. "Is that warning for here?"

"Yes," said one woman, who was calmly buying a pack of gum. "They say if it hits, it will be around three thirty."

It was 2:30. No one was leaving. Outside, the denizens of PG, a small fishing village, went about their business at their usual leisurely pace. I found Moody in front of a case of chocolate from a local cacao farm and alerted him to the television's news crawl. We decided it was best to be on our way to mountainous Fallen Stones, but that we still had time to stop for bread.

On my trip with the Stratford group, I had met a guide who said a man named Gomier made the best bread in Belize. Moody pointed out that the guide was German, so it might be the kind of bread that only Germans like—dark, dense, and heavy. We opted to give it a try anyway.

The sign for Gomier's vegan, vegetarian, and seafood read "Health Is Wealth" over faded red, green, and yellow stripes. The small restaurant sat across the street from the sea, which would have seemed more inviting without the tsunami warning in effect.

Gomier was as tall and lanky as a wind puppet. He had dreads piled high into a crocheted mushroom of a Rasta cap. His first words of greeting were, "You heard they lifted the warning?"

A news alert on my phone flashed the same information several minutes behind Gomier, who, apparently, knew people. Belize was in the clear, although they were still evacuating high-rises in Florida.

Gomier said he had bread coming out of the oven in a half hour. We ordered juices and waited, relieved to be out of evacuation mode. He brought out freshly blended soursop-golden-plum-starfruit juice and joined us for a glass at an outdoor picnic table.

The three of us gazed at the serene blue sea that, just moments before, had felt threatening.

Gomier said the last time there had been a tsunami warning it had come after an earthquake that made his house sway. Except he had been really high at the time and didn't realize it was an earthquake. He thought the tremor was in his head, and he went to bed. Then people started knocking on his door.

"Gomier, get up, get up, there's a tsunami warning!" they shouted.

"It's three a.m.," Gomier shouted back. "If a tsunami comes, it can wash me away in my bed."

I hadn't showed enough imagination in my "think of everything that could go wrong" stage. I'd forgotten tsunamis.

Once we had our loaf of bread (it was hefty, but it smelled delicious), we drove to Hickatee, a few miles outside of town. The propane refrigerator was also in the shipment that hadn't arrived. Alli was sending us up with a big ice chest. She told us not to expect too much at the house. She had hired Sebastian's daughter to clean, but Marthe had had just one day. Alli had tried to outfit the house. But she'd only had time to go to one store.

When I opened the kitchen door, my mouth dropped open. The bugs were gone. Everything was scrubbed. There were cutting boards and knives and drinking glasses, and a pasta strainer (which I'd forgotten on my list!). My favorite part was the four dish towels—red, blue, yellow, and tan—that were neatly hung in a cheery display over a chair.

Moody held up an Aquarius mug—how did Alli know my birthday?

I was in a daze walking up the stairs to the house. I'd barely even noticed the bats in their usual corner on the outside wall.

There were no bats inside. There was a vase of heliconia, commonly called lobster claw, that would amaze me by staying fresh for a month. The bracts—yes, shaped like lobster claws—were orange with wavy stripes of pale green and yellow on the margins. It was easy to see where Alli had found them; they grew like streamers, hanging down from nearby plants that had huge ribbed leaves like the banana trees they're related to.

The bouquet sat on a beautiful table that I hadn't noticed before because it had been outside and covered in butterfly nets. Now that the walls were clean, the concrete showed variations like it belonged in some Napa restaurant that would claim the look was "*rustique*."

Alli had rearranged the furniture to open up the space. There were even hangers on wooden dowels for our clothes. I looked in the bathroom. There was a new sink.

The bedspread was brown and shiny. It wouldn't have been Alli's or my first choice. But Moody and I had somewhere to sleep and linens on the way.

The best improvement of all was the view. Sebastian had the brush cleared, and from the balcony, we could look out and see the valley and mountains and, nearer to the house, soursop, banana, mango, and avocado trees. Dozens of bright-orange *Dryas iulia* butterflies (commonly called Julia) zipped in and out of mounds of orange lantana. A drowsy brown lizard hung vertically on a nearby tree trunk.

Sebastian's brother Bernaldo, one of the groundskeepers, helped us unload. He waved us off and, by himself, carried the filled four-foot ice chest on his shoulder down the stone staircase as if it were a shoebox. Another of their brothers was an electrician. He had hooked up the old solar panels, and they still worked. At night, we would have lights. We could even charge a phone by climbing an indoor ladder, poking our head through a trap door to the attic, and turning on a whining inverter until it complained too loudly.

From the balcony that night, we watched the sky turn sunset fuchsia and then darken. We clinked Belikins, the national beer of Belize, in a toast to our new adventure. It was worth every mosquito bite.

It had been my intention, upon arrival, to never leave the house after dark. I'd been thinking that I would spend the days at the butterfly farm soaking up as much information as possible, then drink my gin and lock up tight after the men who worked there left for the day.

That was thrown out the window that very first night. Moody wanted to look at the world under the stars from the top of that hill. Surprisingly, I did too.

We'd only gone a few yards when Moody started exclaiming: "Wow. Amazing. Can you see *that*?"

I was keeping a close eye out for animal eyes, and I was sticking very close behind Moody. But I didn't know what he was talking about.

"Diana, how can you not see it? There are millions of them," he said.

I wanted a more specific description. He said he was looking at "a dazzling glow like the shining crystals of a fresh frost." I was looking at dark jungle. Moody went closer to investigate and discovered a spider. We crouched down, and I, too, could see the spider. But nothing that looked phosphorescent to him or me.

It wasn't until a couple of days later that we figured out an explanation. I couldn't find my flashlight and grabbed Moody's headlamp to go to the kitchen. As soon as I left the house, I saw a constellation of greenish pin lights in the bushes and all along the trail.

We pondered and theorized that light must be hitting spider eyes and bouncing back, and a person could only see it if your eyes were close to the light source, like when wearing a headlamp.

I consulted the Internet and Sebastian, and both sources confirmed we were right. Like most things, what you saw depended on the angle from which you were looking.

Comfortingly, I was told there weren't as many spiders as there were lights hiding in the jungle. Most spiders have eight eyes, and in some species, four of those eyes have an iridescent layer behind their retinas called a tapetum. It's a common structure in animals that hunt. When light hits the eyes, it bounces off the tapetum and onto the retina, making the hunter better able to see in the dark. It also makes their eyes shine. Think of a cat. Or four of eight spider eyes.

At the top of the mountain that night, and many nights after, Moody and I looked out at the lights of the village and the distant sea. The stars in the sky glittered like the stares of spiders.

Seven

Post-it Notes

Butterfly school started right away. The first lesson wasn't pretty.

I took Moody down to see the latest addition to the Fallen Stones roster, the delicate striped butterflies that Sammy was breeding. On the way, I told Moody the story of how they'd had to let the first butterfly go because they couldn't find the right plant, and how Sammy dreamed of discovering unknown butterfly species.

When we arrived at the right butterfly house, the butterflies weren't there.

We found Sebastian and asked him where they were.

He said they were dead.

Early one morning, the army ants had come. They're called army ants for a reason. They march in regiments. They attack in organized fronts. They can easily kill a scorpion. They can even kill a person if that person can't get out of the way.

They'd engineered their way into the cage. By the time the workers arrived, all that was left were pieces of wings on the ground and two living butterflies. Sammy had to start over with the pupae he had hanging in the butterfly house.

There was a new flight cage outside of the hut. It was tall and narrow like a phone booth, and its four legs stood in wide dishes of water: moats to foil the ants, a protection of ingenuity.

My other butterfly training in the early days of our stay was formal. Sebastian and I sat on the balcony. I had a bright-teal hard-covered notebook and a pen with smooth black ink. Writing things by hand helps me remember them. I recalled sitting on the floor of an air-conditioned bookstore carefully choosing a cool tone for the journal's cover. Its pages were now warm. Everything was warm, me included.

Sebastian dictated the names of the butterfly host plants:

"*Heliconia m-a-r-i-a-e*—the plant with big ribbed leaves by the house. It's for the feeding of the *Caligo memnon* butterfly."

This formal tutelage was how Sebastian had learned from Ray Harberd. They had sat on the same balcony, probably in the same chairs, and Ray had taught Sebastian by dictating the Latin names of butterflies and plants.

Sebastian had only needed the names. From the time he was a young boy, he had observed the natural world around him. He knew which adult butterflies fed on which plants and what their caterpillars ate. He knew where they laid their eggs and how long they lived. Sebastian had a talent for watching.

Before coming to work for Ray, he'd worked on the banana plantations and in citrus and forestry. But those jobs were low paying and got him no closer to his dream of going to school and working for an environmental organization.

He'd turned to cultivating marijuana, a crop that could make money for a person who didn't own land but knew the jungle.

Sebastian's life was then tumbled by forces far beyond him. Newly established Belize (it wasn't a fully independent country until 1981) relied on US and Canadian aid. Those countries funneled money to Belize to fund the police and military as part of the "War on Drugs."

In sparsely populated Belize, officials seldom went up against the organized, violent cartels. They focused their antidrug efforts on village farmers. Sebastian was arrested for growing marijuana and spent two years in a prison the size of an elementary school with a bunch of other farmers he'd known since second and third grade. He held that Belize had imprisoned Maya in exchange for foreign money.

After Sebastian had been freed, he heard rumors in the village of an Englishman living in a ravine by the cattle.

Sebastian thought to himself that the man must be there for a reason. He went out to talk to him. The man living in a tent was Ray Harberd. He was surveying the land to build the road up to what would become a butterfly farm.

Sebastian asked for a job. Ray agreed. Sebastian remembers him saying "I am going to need someone smart and someone who can speak Kekchi and English like you."

Sebastian became Ray's right-hand man as they hired men from the village to build the road, the butterfly farm, and a small resort.

One day, Ray said to him, "Sebastian, I can't afford to pay you for the extra time, but if you want to come here on your day off, I will teach you everything I know."

Sebastian went to Ray's every Sunday. He took books home and read them every night. Now, learned entomologists would occasionally show up in PG asking how to find Sebastian Shol. He had been able to take the vocabulary and scientific knowledge he learned from Ray and combine it with the knowledge passed down from his culture and what he learned living in the jungle to create his own special expertise.

Sebastian had been a better student than me. I could memorize the names and descriptions. But when Sebastian pointed to a real-life thing and asked me to name it, I was consistently stumped.

I would try out all the names I had learned until I hit the right one, the way that when I hold out a tasty morsel for my dog Murphy, he will sit-down-speak-sneeze, running through his whole bag of tricks, hoping to hit upon the right answer.

There were just a few plants that I learned right away.

The *Heliconia collinsiana* has big banana-tree-type leaves. The leaves' undersides are covered with a waxy white substance. The crew called it the chalkboard plant. You could wet a finger and write on the leaves. Which I did. I started by drawing a heart for Moody on a plant near the house. It took him a day to notice, and then he said, "I wonder what lizard made those marks." I went on to inscribe random leaves with such things as "Gold!" with an accompanying pointing arrow. No one ever noticed that I know of, but it amused me.

I could remember the name of the gumbo-limbo trees because it sounded like a dance song and also because they called the trees with their peeling red bark "the tourist tree," and that reminded me to wear sunscreen.

There were twelve employees at the farm, all chosen by Sebastian, working rotating schedules so there was someone caring for the butterflies seven days a week. Moody and I were still learning their names. In the mornings, Moody would go down to the kitchen to make coffee as everyone arrived for the workday. A man carrying a huge bundle of leaves would pass the house. Moody would call out a "good morning," and a chat of mutual curiosity would unfold. I liked to lie in bed and eavesdrop, then get up and peek out the open window to see who I'd been listening to.

Slowly, I started putting the names and voices together. Anselmo was the one who asked a lot of questions and gave a slow and thoughtful "yes" to each of Moody's replies.

Nestor was shy, radiating goodwill and discomfort with every exchange. He was the shortest, so with his bundle of four-foot *Heliconia collinsiana*, he looked like he was emerging from thick foliage.

Santiago, with the round face, had once worked in a restaurant in the cays and been cheated out of his tips. Another time, he had signed on for a construction job building casitas for a would-be resort, and they'd dumped him along with a boatload of men on an uninhabited, bug-infested islet with crates of bottled water and a bag of stale sandwiches, and picked them up two weeks later. He told these stories with laughter, explaining how the restaurant employees had banded together to hide tips and how the construction project went unfinished because his crew didn't do the work and then warned most every worker in Belize about the bad employers so they couldn't hire another crew.

During my study sessions with Sebastian, I learned that the butterflies of each species had a particular host plant where they laid their eggs. The caterpillars hatched and fed on the youngest, most tender leaves. Each man gathered the leaves specific to the species in his particular care, different aged leaves for different stages of caterpillars. Then everyone on the team gathered leaves from the ant leaf tree—the feeding plant for the eating machines known as blue morpho caterpillars. The Belizean common name of *Platymiscium yucatanum* was, unfortunately, apropos, as the glossy leaves were crawling with three types of ants: red ones, black ones, and little black ones. As far as I could tell, they all bit. The tree was called *sanqil che* in Kekchi.

Sanqil sounded a little like Sanka, which is a little like coffee. I made that winding connection to the morning coffee chats and learned my first Kekchi word.

Very quickly, Sebastian and I realized that we should dump the notebook and dutiful stenography and opt instead for daily walks. This benefitted us both, as it was becoming readily apparent from Harvard to the jungle house that I am not a good classroom learner, and with our new arrangement, Sebastian didn't need to set time apart from his day. I could trail after him as he visited flight cages, checked on plants, and studied wild butterflies to compare their behavior to the ones they were breeding. Moody came on an early trek, and I was delightedly stunned to hear him, for the first time, do something that sat squarely in my domain: engage in chatter.

Unprompted, he told Sebastian about the pair of parrots he'd seen at the top of the hill, and striped lichen that looked like layered mushrooms. And a really weird flower that was like a balloon. Like a human organ. Like something beating, he said.

Sebastian nodded.

"As you will see, sir, the jungle is an astonishing place," he said.

The simple statement became our catchphrase.

With each new discovery we reported to one another, there came the invariable reply: "As you can see, sir, the jungle is an astonishing place."

At the end of our first week at the jungle house, Moody and I headed down the trail from the house to the farm. I called this stretch Hummingbird Tunnel. The dirt path was lined with *Justicia aurea*, tall plants with cones of feathery yellow flowers that hummingbirds love. A long-tailed hermit hummingbird buzzed so close to my head that the race-car roar of its wings made me jump.

We turned left just before the blue morpho flight cage and up the trail, which led to the low-slung concrete building that housed Sebastian's office. Along this stretch, Sebastian had planted Santa Maria, a flowering plant that he said could be used to treat snakebite. It was clear he thought it was a good idea to have a lot of it. I managed to commit that one to memory.

Our intention was to see if Sebastian wanted to hike to the waterfall. It was a beautiful destination now that water still flowed but the rainy season had ended. However, Sebastian had suggested we ask for a guide whenever we left the relatively cleared areas around the house and farm buildings.

"I think, Miss Diana, that Mr. Clive would be upset if something happened to you," he had told me.

I was in agreement with Mr. Clive. Especially since the Santa Maria plants were there for a reason.

Our request would require diplomatic gymnastics because we didn't want to be too underfoot or ask for too much time, so we would be trying to feel out the situation, and Sebastian was never direct.

He never once told me he was busy. Instead, he'd tell me it seemed like a nice day for me to sit on the balcony and use the binoculars.

"Good morning," Sebastian said when he saw us. "I was thinking, perhaps sometime you would want to go to my village."

We both agreed that was something we'd very much like to do.

"If you wished, we could drive in the Jeep with my bicycle for me to ride up the next day," he said.

Moody and I said that sounded like a fine plan.

"Today," said Sebastian. "I must go down the hill to meet the bus in Dump at three p.m. A breeder sends me pupae of a butterfly we don't breed here."

I was interested to know that Sebastian occasionally worked with smaller, trusted breeders. I'd find out later that it was his way to help struggling families stay afloat and boost the variety of butterflies he was sending to Stratford. Moody and I both gracefully took the cue to abandon plans for the waterfall. I was disappointed.

"Since it's so close to the end of the working day, I won't be coming back today," Sebastian said.

We nodded our understanding.

The conversation ground to a halt. We all continued to nod and look at one another. Strangely, it didn't seem like the conversation was over. Then it hit me what Sebastian might possibly be proposing, if one carefully put the clues together.

"Mr. Sebastian—do you mean today? Would you like us to put you and your bicycle in the Jeep and we could take you to meet the bus, then visit the village and drop you off at home?"

"I think this might be a very good idea, Miss Diana," said Sebastian, the person who had thought of it.

Once we were all in and buckled up, bicycle included, Moody began his first drive down the mountain. Before we arrived in Belize, I had suspected that I'd be traveling down to Hickatee every other day for a real shower and one of Alli's parakeet breakfasts (scrambled eggs with red and green peppers and onions—her trick being to salt the vegetables first before adding the eggs). But the first week had gone by as if it were one day. I liked pineapple for breakfast, and even enjoyed the outdoor bucket shower that Moody had rigged up, where we warmed water in a teakettle, then poured it through a funnel over our heads. So, with Sebastian, it was our first trip down the mountain.

"You have to remember going uphill is no problem," Moody advised himself aloud as he turned on the engine. "It's going down that's the big problem. Especially if it's rained."

It had rained all night. It rained most nights. I recalled that Alli had told us to put the Hickatee address on the car rental form and never breathe a word about Fallen Stones, as it wasn't a drive that was kind to automobiles or approved of by those who insure them.

We started down the first incline, which pitched the Jeep forward as steeply as an amusement-park ride.

"You should take this part slow but don't hit the brakes too hard," Sebastian said from the back seat.

On the next stretch, the road was not much wider than the Jeep, with steep drop-offs on both sides.

"I hand-carried rocks for this part when we were building the road," said Sebastian. "I think you should drive a little to the left."

The back of the Jeep fishtailed on the mud.

"Easy, Mr. Jack. It is best to keep your wheels straight here," Sebastian said.

Moody hit the brakes.

"Sebastian, you know this road better than anyone. Would you like to drive, and I could learn by watching you?" Moody asked with an edge of hope.

"Oh, I can't do that," Sebastian said.

"Why not?" asked Moody.

"I don't drive," said Sebastian.

When we rolled into San Pedro Columbia, the land flattened out some, and so did our three sets of shoulders. With a population of about eight hundred, it is one of the biggest Mayan villages. There is a Catholic church in the center of town that Sebastian said was made out of stones from the Mayan ruins. Maybe a temple.

"We recycle," he said. The date carved near a door was 1952, but if Sebastian is right, the stones had been cut in the Mayan Classical era (250 to 900 CE).

There were many other churches of various denominations, some just tin and frond one-room shacks with hand-painted signs announcing their respective deity's love.

"We have many churches. We must be very good people," Sebastian said.

The Columbia River ran through town. Families lined the banks and waded in the river washing clothes. I'd also noticed washing machines outside many of the houses.

"This is to show that we are rich enough to buy washing machines," said Sebastian. "But the electricity to make them run is too much money."

The village was picturesque. Huts with thick thatch roofs sat on round green hills. The roads were dirt and mainly traveled by people on foot. Some families had a traditional hut of thatch and a second structure of concrete block that wouldn't blow away in a hurricane. Many chose to sleep in the thatch because it was cooler and cook in the concrete because it was less flammable. Others did the opposite: cooked in the thatch because it was cooler and slept where the walls were sturdier. Yet others had split the difference and taken the best of both structures, building concrete block houses with thatched roofs.

Some of the women we passed wore traditional dress: square-necked dresses with lace trim and puffy sleeves, or a lace-trimmed blouse with a colorful Mayan skirt. But there were also women in yoga pants. We passed a young couple on a moped. The girl on the back wore a striped sundress and a baseball cap. The boy was wearing madras shorts.

It was quiet. Many people were working on their farms or jobs in town, and at that time of day, schoolchildren were in class. The oddest part of the village to Moody and me was that, of the people who were out, no one waved.

We passed a man. He looked straight at us with no expression as we drove by. Sebastian looked back at him with no expression.

Moody asked, "Do you know that guy?"

"Oh, yes," said Sebastian. "That is my brother-in-law. He's a very nice man."

So it went as we drove by people Sebastian had known his whole life but whom he felt no need to acknowledge. Not even a nod passed between them. No one greeted one another. Moody said he thought he would have made a very good Mayan village resident. He warned Sebastian not to let me infect San Pedro Columbia with the need to squeal over every acquaintance.

Sebastian directed us to park outside his home, which consisted of both a thatch and a concrete house and a horticulturist's dream yard of fruit trees and flowers. His wife, Hovita, stepped out of the thatch, a slender woman with startling turquoise eyes wearing a T-shirt with a butterfly graphic. Sebastian had told us that Hovita was a cancer survivor and that he worried about her. They'd met when she was a cook during Fallen Stones' long-ago attempt to cultivate the farm into a rustic resort. According to him, it was love at first sight for both of them. According to Marthe, their daughter, Sebastian had come around so many times when her mother was trying to cook that she finally agreed to see him outside of work.

We exchanged quick hellos with Hovita, who was in the middle of cooking, then dropped Sebastian off and continued on our way out of town, passing the hand-lettered sign that pointed to Lubaantun.

Scholars do not draw a direct connection between the Maya in the San Pedro Columbia of today and the ancient Maya of Lubaantun, because Lubaantun was abandoned around 890 CE and San Pedro Columbia was settled almost a thousand years later. The Kekchi were a culturally distinct minority Mayan group from the Verapaz region of Guatemala. In the late 1800s, the Guatemalan government stole the Mayan communal lands and gave them to coffee plantation owners who enslaved the Maya to work their fields. The Kekchi who escaped and made it over the mountains to Belize settled San Pedro Columbia.

San Antonio, the other large Mayan village in Toledo, was settled by Mopan Maya, who also were fleeing abuse in Guatemala.

The Mopan Maya and the Kekchi Maya speak different indigenous languages but share English Kriol (and judging from asking the guys at the farm about their parents and wives, seem to make a habit of marrying one another).

The Kekchi Maya were historically the most impoverished minority group in Belize. But there was a new air of empowerment, part of a pan-Mayan cultural and political uprising. In Belize, families were trying desperately to send their children to school at least beyond eighth grade and hoped for college.

Most families in San Pedro Columbia had little money for buying things, but many owned their own land and houses, had enough food to eat because of subsistence farming, practiced communal child care, and routinely added their voices to local government. They had a type of security and belonging that many American families only dream about.

Even out in what they called the bush, far from paved roads, there was a spirit of progress in isolated villages. Along one remote road, we had come upon a series of hand-painted signs exhorting, "Women Can Be Leaders Too." I felt the "too" gave the thought an unfortunate sound of surprise. But even a generation ago, a Mayan village had been a strictly patriarchal culture.

The third week of our stay at Fallen Stones, one morning under the shade of a coconut tree, Sebastian was showing me how to hang pupae. We were putting evenly spaced dots of rubber cement on a long stick and pressing the chrysalides onto them. The chrysalides would hang in the flight cage until the butterflies emerged.

I asked Sebastian what it had been like when he was growing up in San Pedro Columbia.

"My father died when I was thirteen, and I had no one to look out for me," he told me.

"I was fifteen when my father died," I said.

Sebastian said his father had died from obeah. I had heard the word before. It was black magic.

In the Afro-Caribbean cultures of Belize, there was a movement to reclaim obeah as a spiritual practice brought from Africa by enslaved people and maligned by a white establishment afraid of its powers. In those cultures, obeah was believed to be a force that could be used for good as well as evil.

But in Mayan communities, obeah meant evil. Usually, it was brought on by jealousy. Someone putting a hex on you because they envied something you had, or because they thought you were a little too full of yourself. Just the threat of it was enough to remind you that you'd better keep your head down.

Sebastian said people had been jealous of his father, a hardworking farmer, a provider. One day, his father suddenly got the hiccups. He couldn't stop hiccupping for two days until he had a heart attack and died. The shadow of obeah touched Sebastian and his six siblings' lives forever. With my father, it had been lung cancer, but I figured that the lingering shadow was all the same black magic: an evil force that makes you fear being strong and happy in case, in its jealousy, it takes everything away. When I finished gluing pupae to sticks, it was midafternoon. I headed back to the house. It was the time of day that Moody and I hid inside, still and supine, seeking relief from the heat like most every other jungle creature.

As I walked, I carried a touch of melancholy over the losses. Sebastian's, mine, everyone's.

Somehow that sadness grew into the thought that, in life itself, the odds are against us. There is so much threat, so much grief, and always lurking was the almost-secret knowledge that loved ones will die, that we will die. I could barely breathe as the thought crossed my mind because I knew Kari, my friend in London, was soon starting chemotherapy.

On the other hand, Kari was proof of the immense joy in the small moments. She had recently sent a photo showing her cat, Reilly, sniffing flowering bulbs on the windowsill. Her note said she'd been listening to the song "You Must Believe in Spring"—the Bill Evans and Tony Bennett version, she had specified. She had also written that she had taken a class in the Japanese art of moss balls, which involved coating the roots of a snowball flower (or a harbinger of spring, as she called it) in mud and moss. Picturing her trundling home on the Tube with a big dirt ball almost made me smile despite my worry.

I stopped at the blue morpho flight cage, knowing they would be active at that time of day. Butterflies are ectotherms, meaning they rely on the outside environment for warmth. The blue morphos basked all morning with their wings spread open, soaking in the sunshine. Then when they were warm enough, they flew.

In front of me, dozens of butterflies were in the air, making fluttering, flashing loops of purple and brilliant turquoise. I could even hear them flying, a whhhhhffff that was soft and loud at the same time.

But in my current mood, the scene seemed desperate: this whole complicated undertaking of raising butterflies in flight cages to protect about a hundred acres of rain forest and create a dozen jobs that weren't poisoning or deforesting the jungle, when all around, greater forces of climate change and inequality loomed.

I started back in the clinging heat, swatting at mosquitoes. I saw a flash of blue flying near the yellow *Justicia*. Then another wild blue morpho chasing through the green forest. I could also see a postman butterfly (*Heliconius melpomene*)—black with magenta racing stripes— slowly zigzagging through the passion vines where they lay their eggs.

How lucky I am to see this, I thought. *How lucky to be here.*

I had to laugh at my next thought: What if I had stumbled upon the true purpose of butterflies?

Of course, there was the role of pollinator—key to the entire eco-system and their deep, cultural meanings.

But what if they were also like, well, cosmic Post-it Notes?

Don't forget: be amazed.

To-do: be thankful.

Maybe they were eye-catching reminders that, yes, there are powerful dark forces and heart-wrenching loss, but there is also beauty and color. There is life. So, screw it, don't keep your head down. Soak in any warmth you can find, and then fly.

Eight

ONE TOUCAN

Moody had left me a mug of coffee on the outdoor table. It must be nice to be one of those people who wake effortlessly at dawn.

He had gone up to the top of the hill. I could tell because the binoculars were missing and he liked to watch the parrots at first light.

I sat down, stretched my arms, and picked up the book lying on the railing, *Birds of Belize* by H. Lee Jones. I opened it randomly to the part about how to use the book.

"Ideally the book should not be consulted until *after* the bird has been thoroughly studied, notes taken and sketches made," advised Jones. "The more time spent studying the bird, not the book, while the bird is in view means more time absorbing important information about the bird."

Wow, I thought. *How often does the universe just reach out and hit you on the head with writing advice?*

I decided I would concentrate on just being in this place, this small sanctuary in Belize, *while the bird was in view,* so to speak. Everything else could wait. I perhaps didn't need to memorize insect genera. Moody came down the trail. He was whistling. When we'd initially began dating, my first clue that he wasn't as much of a grouch as I'd previously thought was how often he went around whistling to himself.

"You need to get up there and talk to a guy named Profilio. He's the groundskeeper," he told me as he climbed the stairs to the deck.

"What's it about?" I asked.

"I couldn't even begin to explain," he said.

Less than a month had passed since our arrival, but I'd noticed that the 159 steps up to the top (of course, I counted) were becoming almost easy.

Near the Jeep, I ducked beneath the red-orange flowers of the flamboyant tree. (It was perfectly named—the root of "flamboyant" is old French meaning "wavy fire.")

I found Profilio cutting long grasses on the ridge with a motorized weed whacker. He turned the machine off and walked over to me as soon as I made my way to the top.

"I must make sure there is nothing for fire to consume," he told me.

It was clear that he was game to entertain any audience as he launched into a series of stories. His speaking voice sounded like singing. Pretty much every Belizean, no matter their ethnicity, has a lilting quality to their speech because the lingua franca is Belizean Kriol. It's an English-based language first created by enslaved Africans who were forced to work in the mahogany logging camps. *"Dis da fi we langwidhj, dis da fi we life,"* the motto of the National Kriol Council, means: "This is our language, this is our life." It ties the wild diversity of the country together. The Creoles, Garifuna, Maya, and even the Mennonites with Low German as their first language speak Kriol.

We began learning how universal the Kriol language was when, once or twice a week, Moody and I began driving into PG for groceries. We bought our produce at the daily farmers market, trying to spread our business equally between the stalls of bananas, pineapples, peppers, nuts, rice, and potatoes. Most of the proprietors there were Mayan women who chatted with us and each other in songlike cadences. They rode the bus into town from the countryside carrying their fruits and vegetables. There were also stalls run by Mennonites who brought their produce in horse-drawn wagons. The first time we bought a watermelon from a decidedly white Mennonite with a bowl haircut and suspenders named Walter, I had been surprised when he started to tell us about his farm in a Caribbean patois. But, of course, he did. He was Belizean.

Even though I had started to expect that melodic quality, I was mesmerized by Profilio, whose speech particularly danced. Maybe because words rolled and jumbled out of him as he tried to keep up with the thoughts that rolled and jumbled inside of him. Everything he said was delivered with fevered zeal.

Moody would come to dub Profilio the Belizean John Muir, after the naturalist who described the beauty of the Sierra mountains as if he had been beamed to Earth from another realm.

Profilio said Mr. Jack had told him that I'd be interested in the silk-cotton tree.

"This is the tree Lady Isabella taught me to obtain its secrets," he said. "Lady" was a title of respect for older women in the village.

Lady Isabella was his grandmother, and she had died that same day.

Profilio had suffered emotional problems in the past. He had faint scars on his arms that looked like they may have been self-inflicted years ago.

"Sometimes we have great turbulence and feel lost," he said.

Lady Isabella had taught him ways to calm his mind.

One of the things Lady Isabella had told him was that he should sleep on a pillow made from the fluff of the tree where the yellowtail most liked to roost.

The yellowtail, or Montezuma Oropendolas, arrived on the top of the hill each evening. They were big birds who traveled in a flock and made a fuss as they settled in to roost on the tall silk-cotton, or ceiba, trees that spread out against the sky like pagodas.

I foolishly had not paid close attention to birds before, but in Belize, they had become our Netflix. The Oropendola has pale-blue patches around its eyes, a purplish-bronze chest, and as the common name advertises, a yellow tail. They made an eerie noise that started as a high-pitched note and ended with a sound like crumpling paper. You could see them silhouetted on the cotton trees at sunset as if they were part of the tree's crown.

These trees produced fruit at irregular times, not tied to a certain season. When a breeze came, it blew down the fruit that then split open and sent hundreds of seeds floating away on silky fibers.

Lady Isabella had told Profilio to carry a cotton flour sack and collect the loose fibers for a pillow.

She said, "Just one sleep on this pillow, and you will have the answers for those obstacles that can sometimes seem so puzzling."

"You know how life can go," Profilio said. "The world can seem so in turmoil, where your feet walk is in turmoil, there seems no way out."

He had followed his grandmother's instructions and collected the fibers until he had enough for a pillow. It took him months.

"Then I laid my head down on my little pillow and slept well, and when I woke up in the morning, I felt like a conqueror," he said. "I become more open to people. I started talking."

There was a time Profilio didn't talk, my mind noted in shock. It must have been deep turmoil to silence someone as ebullient as Profilio.

Profilio said the pillow helped him feel "communal wisdoms from the past of how to jump through obstacles." He said he thought it was because the pillow came from nature and his own efforts instead of just walking into a store to buy it. "The pillow holds the soft substance the tree put out in the world, and the times I gathered it in my little bag. It reminds me that we're all connected in this universe," he said.

He lost that pillow in the big hurricane, and the storm felled the ceiba trees he'd used to gather the fibers.

When the trees grew back at the higher elevations, Profilio did something he didn't think would work. He collected their seeds and planted one in his yard in the village. It grew. People often stopped to look at the tree now, because aracari, small black toucans with rainbow-colored chests and beaks, congregate there. Someday, he said, he will make another pillow. But for now, the birds are eating most of the fruit from his young tree before it falls.

We had started walking while we talked. The former bar, from the days when the farm was meant to function as an eco-resort, was on the ridge overlooking the canyon. Sebastian had warned Moody and me not to go inside. It was termite chewed and a hazard about to tumble down the cliff. Profilio showed me a spot just off the walkway to the building that was good for animal watching.

The day before, he had been there eating his lunch when a deer passed by. He sat very still, silently telling the deer that he meant her no harm.

"She shook her little tail and did her ears like this," he said, holding up his hands and bending his fingers forward. "That's a language. It's so unique, the animal language. She said hello to me."

The jungle we were looking over seemed dense and ancient to me. But I kept being reminded that it was new. Once, mahogany trees, several hundred feet tall and several hundred years old, had towered here. But when Hurricane Iris hit, it uprooted even the majestic trunks and trademark buttresses of old-growth mahogany. I was used to a huge scale of devastation with the California wildfires. I understood that, to me, the scene was green and lush, but that Sebastian and the others would always compare it to a lost landscape.

Many people outside of Belize have never heard of Hurricane Iris. It's not one of those famous storms of wide destruction, but it was a direct hit on Southern Belize.

In late September 2001, a tropical wave formed outside of Barbados and began traveling through the Caribbean Sea. A low pressure system developed. The winds near the Lesser Antilles pointed it in the direction of Belize. After it passed Jamaica, the storm gained power and speed.

On October 8, as the rest of the world grappled with the aftermath of 9/11 and the drumbeats of war, Hurricane Iris hit Belize's southern coast with 145-mile-per-hour winds. The sea surged eighteen feet.

The *Wave Dancer*, a luxury diving boat that had been sheltering at a concrete pier in Big Creek, was ripped from its moorings and overturned. Seventeen of twenty members of a dive club from Richmond, Virginia, and three of eight of the Belizean crew, were killed. One survivor was tossed into a mangrove three hundred feet away.

The hurricane tore into the interior of the country. Its diameter was small, and the winds stretched only fifteen miles from the center of the storm, but it uprooted everything in its path.

San Pedro Columbia and the smaller Mayan villages in Toledo were destroyed, their thatched houses blown apart. The forest was razed. This wild space and these resilient people were still in recovery twenty years later.

Sebastian had told me about trying to find Fallen Stones the next day. There was nothing familiar to guide him. The road was completely covered; the trees were gone.

When he finally reached the farm, he found that nothing was left. The house where Moody and I were living now had a thatch roof in those days. It was blown away. The flight cages were gone, their butterflies dead and gone. The wild butterflies were gone too. Their delicate wings could not survive the powerful winds.

There was only one thing left. During the days that the radio had been blaring hurricane warnings, Sebastian had packed a box. In that box, he put six hundred pupae from different species. He put the box in the only concrete building at the farm, the one that housed his office. He surrounded the box with heavy cement blocks and put one block on top.

When they returned, the blocks were there. He pushed and heaved them aside. The box was there. The pupae were safe. Two weeks later, there were eggs; soon after that, there were caterpillars.

The hurricane hadn't left a single leaf at Fallen Stones to feed the caterpillars. But, back then, the farm had an old truck that had seen better days. Workers drove to San Antonio, San Felipe, and PG to find trees that had been spared, gather leaves, and drive them back to San Pedro Columbia where they left the truck. From there, the workers put the leaves on their backs and hiked to the farm because the road was impassible to vehicles or bicycles. Almost every butterfly at Fallen Stones traces back to those six hundred pupae that Sebastian saved.

With the forest upended, the villagers and the animals who depended on it had little food. It was during this time that Profilio told me he'd had his most intense communion with an animal.

The howler monkeys had come down close to the village, which they would never do under normal circumstances. "They were longing for what we were all longing for—a little something in the pot, a little something in the belly," he said.

Profilio was crouched outside eating a bowl of cereal that relief workers had distributed. A howler monkey sat very close to him, and he tossed it little pieces of the food.

"We had no language in common, but our eyes met and we told each other about our hopelessness," he said.

With the trees gone, grasses grew on the mountains, changing the landscape. The rainy season passed. The heat came and dried the grasses.

"They were waiting for one spark," Profilio said.

The hurricane had destroyed the corn crop. Other villages sent seeds so San Pedro Columbia could replant. Some of the Mayan farmers still practice slash-and-burn farming, a method of farming where they purposely set fires to clear a field enough to plant. To get one acre of farmland, they sometimes burn about three acres of forest.

That was the spark. One of the fires escaped. It was unstoppable. Fire went everywhere the wind blew.

Sebastian had told me about the day it reached Fallen Stones. They had been watching it in the distance, hoping it would turn. Then, suddenly, it was on them and they were running for their lives.

At the top of the hill, propane tanks flew into the air and exploded with huge bangs and bursts of fire. The crew grabbed their bicycles and pedaled furiously down the steep road. Their vision was obscured by thick, dark smoke. They didn't slow until they reached the river.

Once again, Ray had been in England and had heard of the catastrophe from afar. He flew back immediately, arriving three days after the disaster. The fire had somehow burned everywhere except the butterfly house at the bottom of the valley and the old growth near the waterfall. Fallen Stones sent a shipment to Stratford that week.

Profilio wasn't working at Fallen Stones then. He was still the new guy—Sebastian had hired him five months before I'd arrived.

He hoped someday to advance from groundskeeping to caring for the butterflies, but he said that his current job as the groundskeeper was important because he cut the grass and weeds very low around the trail and buildings, so if fire came, he and the others would have a chance to turn it away from the farm.

We were walking back to where he'd left off his weeding when he stopped and pointed at a toucan in a trumpet tree.

"I'm so glad he made it back to the sanctuary! I saw him fly off a few days ago. They kill them for their beaks," he said. "I used to think this place was only about butterflies. But every day, I see something new and learn the place is for many creatures. When they leave, I worry, and I welcome them when they return."

Profilio's face was turned up looking at the tree and the bird. His eyes were alight.

"Sometimes I will be given to worry about a lot of things. I saw there is talk of war today. There is global warming, and corrupt people misuse our natural resources," he said. "But you can see one toucan—one!—and it changes your way of thinking. It gives hope."

When I got back to the house, Moody said, "Well?"

I opened my mouth to speak and found I couldn't. There was a strange tugging of tears at my outer eyes. I pressed my lips hard together. I tried again to speak and failed again.

"Yeah," said Moody. "I know."

Nine

CLOSE TO HOME

Somewhere out there, beyond the forest and the villages, was tourist Belize. I had expected to have more interest in it. But now that I was being tutored on how to observe more closely, the world immediately around me was taking all of my attention. Below the deck, attached to the house, was a wax cone entrance to a stingless Meliponini beehive. Every evening, the bees, looking like tiny flying ants, returned to the nest and closed themselves in with a perforated wax curtain over the front of the cone. Pretty much like Moody and I did in the house above. There were always a few bees buzzing outside the cone. I thought they were latecomers who got locked out, but a 2011 study at the University of Sussex revealed some of the hive's bees are specifically assigned night-time guard duty.

I had made peace with the bats as soon as Sebastian told me they ate mosquitoes. But I did still encourage them to leave before I went down to get drinks and snacks from the kitchen in the evening.

"Why are you still here?" I'd ask, poking my head slightly out the door. "The bat discos are open. Romance is in the air. *Fly away.*"

In the mornings, I'd visit the various butterfly houses, no doubt making a pest of myself. I would try to help with feeding caterpillars or counting eggs or packing.

The Fallen Stones' entire system of raising butterflies was ingenious.

It started with counting the butterfly eggs—a task that's harder than it sounds. Felipe, who worked in the same building as Sebastian, and had been friends with him since childhood, showed me how.

Butterfly eggs are tiny and irregularly scattered on a leaf, so it's tricky to remember which ones you already counted. If my mind wandered for even a second, I lost count and had to start over.

Felipe taught me to use a pen to mark the leaf and create groupings. Then to make scratch marks of the count on my hand. There wasn't much he could do about my wandering mind, but the system helped me get back on track more quickly.

Sometimes, Manuel and Malvin, the two youngest on the staff, would lurk, waiting until Felipe looked very deep in concentration, then they would take turns walking in and asking a question, making him lose count, over and over again, until a distracted Felipe finally caught on to them. Once, I even spotted Sebastian laughing at the prank.

After the butterfly eggs were counted, the leaves, and thus the eggs, went in a wooden box. The boxes were old and beautifully crafted like little treasure chests. I wished I had a stack of them at home. The eggs of a species were often color coordinated to the butterfly as well as to the host plant. The malachite butterfly, with its black and neon-green wings, laid bright-green eggs on the underside of the youngest leaves of the Belizean sage plant, which flew flags of red-orange flowers. The malachite caterpillar was black and red orange, the exact same shade as those flowers.

The blue morpho eggs were translucent, able to pass as a dewdrop, so they held a hint of the iridescence to come. They took up to twelve days to hatch and subtly changed color each day. If the egg was fertilized, it developed a dot of black in the middle. Outside that was a ring of brownish-black dashes that echoed the intricate patterns on the closed wings of a morpho.

Butterfly books often describe the bottom side of blue morpho wings as dull brown, which I don't see. Yes, they have a woody-brown backdrop, but there is a coral ridge on the outer edge, and the eyespots, meant to mimic the look of a predator's eyes, are purplish black with a ring of yellow, then a black border, and around that, a wavy white stripe. They're spectacular—unless compared to the other side of brilliant blue.

Every detail of a butterfly's markings seemed to mean something. Sebastian said that if a morpho's dorsal wings have a black border with two rows of white dots, it's male. The slightly smaller butterflies with a thinner black border on their wings are female. Once in a great while, a butterfly would hatch with one male and one female wing, and Sebastian would be very excited to see the variation.

Dame Rothschild, the flea expert who had cheered on the creation of Clive's butterfly house, had studied the meanings of butterfly colors. She was part of a team that was looking to prove that some butterflies were toxic because they ate plants that are poisonous to their predators. She continued on to show that through color-coding that's common in nature, the butterflies' bright colors advertised their toxicity and kept their predators away. But other butterflies that weren't toxic evolved to mimic those bright colors and fake out predators.

Probably the most famous toxic butterfly is the orange-and-black monarch. The monarch caterpillar eats poisonous milkweed that makes it poisonous and stays in the system of the adult butterfly. If a bird eats one, it doesn't die, but it throws up. Word gets around, and the other monarchs are protected.

One day, Nestor was in my morning walk-and-learn sights. He worked alone in a little shack with the *Caligo memnon* butterflies—a less flashy cousin of the morphos. The common name is owl butterfly because of the big eye pattern on its wings. They were the first butterflies to fly in the mornings and the last butterflies to fly at night.

"Hi, Nestor. Are you busy?" I asked from the doorway.

"My words are not busy. Only my hands," he said. Nestor was feeding caterpillars. All caterpillars start eating leaves as soon as they hatch and don't stop until they are ready to spin a chrysalis.

To feed the caterpillars as Nestor and I were doing, we had to take down one of the wooden boxes. Each box had caterpillars from eggs that had been laid on the same day.

We removed the leaves and caterpillars from the box we were working on and sat them on the table. We turned over the box and dumped out the chewed leaves and the caterpillars' waste, which looked like sand. We brushed out the box, then put in some supporting sticks, propping them horizontally between the sides of the box. We added fresh leaves, arranging them so it would be easy for a caterpillar to get from one to the other.

Using tweezers, if the caterpillars were tiny, or my fingers, if they were the big ones and I didn't want to look squeamish, even though I kind of was, I plucked the caterpillars off the old leaves and put them on the fresh leaves in the box.

Different stages of caterpillars need different stages of a leaf. Young caterpillars eat young, tender leaves. It took eight hundred varying heliconia leaves to feed the *Caligo* each day. The farm's voracious blue morpho caterpillars went through seventy-five pounds of *sanqil che* leaves each day.

As we worked, I asked Nestor about his family. He had a house full. Eight children, including mischievous two-and-a-half-year-old twins, Jalon and Junior.

"Either I have too much or they are God's blessing," he said. "I think it's the last one. I'm so thankful for them."

I knew from Sebastian that the twins were born after Nestor and his wife had lost one of their older children.

After I finished the boxes with Nestor, I wandered over to say hello to Anselmo and Julio, who worked in a different shack feeding blue morpho caterpillars.

They were outside on a log, using razor blades to scrape caterpillar hairs out of their arms and hands. Caterpillars go through five stages where they shed their exoskeleton and emerge in a slightly altered form. In a blue morpho, each stage, or instar (from the Latin "*instar*," meaning "form"), is quite different, and the last one is a doozy.

They start out as furry little things that you can brush with your finger to no ill effect. But, the fifth instar larvae gave me the creeps. They were almost four inches long, reptilian looking, but with tufts of rust-colored spiny hairs that irritated human skin. If you touched a fifth instar near its thorax, it emitted a foul, rancid smell, like butter gone bad. It wasn't all flying flowers in the butterfly business.

The toxic hairs floated around the shack and settled in Anselmo's and Julio's clothes and skin. They had tried measures to mitigate the effect, like wearing gloves and long sleeves, but the extra protection made the work too hot and clumsy. They could slightly calm the stinging itch by scraping out the hairs once their work was done.

On that day, they had brought a small transistor radio for entertainment. They were listening to Latin dance music. Julio said he loved dancing *cumbia*. He'd picked it up working at a bar on Caye Caulker in the north when he was younger.

Anselmo said he liked country music. I thought that meant the music of his country. I laughed and told him I liked country music too, but the cowboy-boot kind. He said that was exactly what he was talking about.

"Brad Paisley, Garth Brooks," he said.

"I've got some music for you!" I said, whipping out my phone. My cousin Scott is a country singer, and you have to promote family when you can. We sat on a Belizean log, listening to my Nashville cousin's "Hey Hillbilly Singer!" Then we switched from old-school country to Latin dance. I coaxed Julio into showing off his *cumbia* skills, and we danced outside by the mango tree.

Before I left the farm, I took a detour up to look at the striped newcomer butterflies that Sammy was breeding. The ant attack had been devastating, but now, every week there were more eggs, more pupae, more floating little butterflies. There was always a vase of fresh flowers inside the telephone-booth flight cage. The blooms were chosen for their appeal to the butterflies, but it looked like a master florist had arranged bright-red waxy hot lips with orange lantana and sprigs of purple *Stachytarpheta*.

When I got back to the house, Moody was on the balcony. He came down the stairs to meet me.

"I just saw the craziest thing," he said.

He'd been watching birds again. Which was not a surprise. Not that Moody would ever admit to being a *bird-watcher*. He saw himself as an outdoorsman who strode through fields pheasant hunting, not some bookish sort with binoculars making check marks on a list. What saved our relationship when he first told me about his pheasant-hunting expeditions was that he also told me what a bad shot he was, and that the birds went unharmed.

But now there were check marks all over the *Birds of Belize* book, and he'd swiped one of my precious notebooks to jot down bird descriptions.

If someone had overheard our dinner conversations, they may have been puzzled as we chirped, whistled, clicked, and croaked, trying to discuss the bird sounds we had heard that day.

On that afternoon, he'd been on the balcony—ahem, bird-watching—when he saw two hawks. One of the hawks had been standing at the very tip of a branch, chewing at a spot nearer the tree. The branch had snapped, and Moody had watched the hawk tumble like a circus performer. The bird had barely stretched out its wings and pulled up at the last minute before it would have crashed into the jungle floor.

"It was like a guy building a house, and he's up high, standing on a two-by-four, sawing behind him," Moody said. "That was one dumb hawk." Moody made it sound like a bird blooper reel.

The workday was over, and Bernaldo, Sebastian's brother, who was in charge of the grounds, walked past us on his way to his bicycle. Moody told him about the bird aeronautics he'd witnessed, and Bernaldo said it was actually a smart hawk. That's how they break the twigs for their nest. They use their weight to weaken the branch. Sebastian came by a little later, and Moody told him about it too.

"So, *that's* what happened," he said in a musing voice. "Remember the other day when you were reading, Miss Diana?" he asked me.

I'd been at the house alone in the afternoon, stretched out with a book, half listening to the constant bird sounds in the background.

Suddenly the jungle had erupted. I'd told Sebastian there had been every kind of screeching and thumping and calling. It was as if a main act had arrived on stage and the audience went nuts. Then, just as suddenly, quiet. More silence than I had heard since arriving.

"The hawks came in from up top," Sebastian said, like Columbo narrating as he pieced together a mystery. "A warning went out. It spread. You heard the uproar. By the time the hawks got here, everybody was quiet and hidden."

Using his book, Moody identified the not-so-dumb hawk as a plumbeous kite (not exactly a hawk, but close).

"Look at his eyes! They're red," he said, waving his now-favorite book in front of me.

"And the call is rapid laughing. It goes like this: hee-h-h-h-he, he," he read aloud, adding that it had a ringing quality, in case I hadn't picked that up from his rendition.

By then, we barely had time to climb the zigzag of stones to make it for sunset up top—a daily ritual we'd adopted—followed by Alli-inspired gin and tonics on the deck. It had taken a very short time for us to consider these things routine, the markers of an ordinary day.

Ancient stones, bats, the Caribbean Sea in the distance, always remembering rubber boots for snake protection, all just part of our current world. I'm always surprised by how quickly former realities fade when I travel.

On top, as we always called it, we listened for the croaks that sounded like frogs but led our eyes to toucans, watched the yellowtail squabble and roost in the cotton tree while the sun dipped behind Guatemala, and then it was time to go home and chide the bats:

"What are you *still* doing here? You have mosquitoes to eat. There's a smorgasbord this evening. All you can eat. I know you have a coupon!"

For more than a month, the days slipped by without us venturing farther afield other than our trips to visit Alli and the boys or shop in PG. Some weeks, we didn't leave the farm at all. We kept a running tab with Alli, and she would send groceries up to us via David, who came on Thursdays to pick up the butterfly box. I always looked forward to David's visits. I think it was because of his big smile and quiet intelligence. But it might have been because he brought us cheese and strawberries and chocolate. When we flipped through a travel book, or a friend recommended an adventure, we invariably had the same reaction: "Maybe when Kat gets here."

Ten

INSTARS

Moody had been saying "When Kat gets to Belize . . ." before we'd even arrived in Belize.

Kat was Moody's Joplin-singing, groovy-print-wearing, creative daughter. If anyone was going to gasp and light up over butterflies, it would be Kat.

Our long-delayed supplies arrived just in time for her visit, including the propane refrigerator that Clive had bought. Moody was grievously disappointed that we had missed seeing the appliance being carried down the hundred-plus stone steps while we were on a trip to PG.

I put the linen sheets on the beds and heliconia in a vase on the table in the long room that separated the matching bedrooms. Kat and I exchanged texts full of smiley emojis and packing tips. I told her the point of clothes in the jungle was to cover as much skin as possible. I didn't want her to make the same mistake I had on our first trip, packing flirty sundresses, better to offer myself up for a bug feast.

I was to take time off from reporting so we could concentrate on showing Kat the farm and then explore more of Belize. The house was filled with happy anticipation.

There was just one shadow on her impending arrival—she'd added the boyfriend to her trip.

As far as I could say, there wasn't anything specifically wrong with Jed, who she lived with in a tiny California mountain town. But the last time Moody visited them, he had overheard the two talking and Kat crying.

"Once you hear your daughter crying . . . ," he said in the tone of a farmer who had seen signs of fungus at harvest time.

The night before their flight, Jed and Kat drove to the airport and slept in Kat's car because they had an early flight and didn't want to miss it. They overslept in the car and missed it.

"Fair enough, I know my daughter," said Moody. "But what's wrong with this guy?" He got them rerouted and bought new tickets for their puddle jumper since it was too late to rebook. They arrived a day later during a perfect sunset.

Moody, who often grumbled his way through life like a put-upon Jimmy Stewart, was as patient as a hunting tree frog when it came to his kids.

"Just think," he said as we watched their little plane circle and land, "if she'd made her flight, she would have landed in rain. But now she gets this sunset."

Jed was a big guy. Thighs like tree trunks. A head taller than six-foot Moody. He had shaggy hair, a pack of cigarettes in his pearl-buttoned shirt pocket, and sandals on his feet.

When Kat looked at him, you could almost hear her eyelashes flutter. She didn't seem to notice that Jed didn't project a similar enthusiasm about anything.

Oh, honey, I couldn't help thinking. *Been there. It isn't pretty.*

Their first morning at the butterfly farm, I sat down next to Jed, who was outside smoking a cigarette.

I asked him about his time as a river guide. He said he'd like to get back on a river, but in the future, he wanted to be the person paddling the canteen boat because that guy didn't have responsibilities—he didn't have to talk to people and could pack beer.

He asked me what we ate at the butterfly farm.

I described the pineapple, mango, and different varieties of banana with zeal. I bragged a bit about the creative meals we'd managed with the basic fare of tomatoes, onions, peppers, beans, and rice that we bought from Mayan women in PG. I only realized later that Jed had suspected correctly that he was among vegetarians and had only wanted to know if there was beef in the new refrigerator. I had figured we could buy their favorite foods after they'd settled in and we made a trip to town.

Then he asked me what we had planned during their stay, which was originally supposed to be ten days.

I mentioned butterfly flight houses and a walk to ancient ruins.

He nodded, took a drag on his cigarette, and said, "And then?"

He asked if I had anything specific planned for Wednesday. What about Friday?

I told him it was Belize and we planned on winging it. He looked thoughtful and took another slow drag.

After a breakfast of fruit and eggs and tortillas, the four of us went inside the flight cages with Sebastian. Kat was incandescent. With all the butterflies clinging to her, she looked like a highly decorative lamp. We retired to the house for the hot part of the day. But Jed and Kat decided to forgo the downtime and walk to the village instead. It was more than three miles. It was hot enough to steam rice. They didn't want a ride. They found a bar, spent the afternoon there, and returned many hours later, exuberant, tipsy, and carrying a big bag of frozen chicken.

That night, we gave them the headlamp and took them on the walk to the top. Not only did they see the greenish-crystal glow of eyes, Jed spotted a spider carrying hundreds of babies on her back, walking along like an animated pincushion.

"Did you see how stoked they were?" Moody asked later, pleased that the spiders had proved a hit.

The morning came with a soft blue sky and wispy clouds that seemed to be stretching out to their fingertips trying to touch the mountains on each side of them (reach, reach, reach).

We took a special walk to visit our nearest neighbors, Richard and Alisa, who lived in an Earthship next to Lubaantun.

Earthships are self-sustaining structures made of recycled materials, or a "madhouse made from rubbish!" as Alisa explained it. The concept is based on the work of New Mexico architect Michael Reynolds, who promotes "radically sustainable living."

Richard and Alisa's place had the voluptuous curves and color of a Gaudí and the exuberance of a kindergarten painting. Bottles were embedded in walls made of cement, trash, and tires. The bottles added light and looked like glowing holes, creating patterns of hearts and suns and irregular shapes.

The first time I saw the place was on my trip with Clive, James, and Sarka. Clive had asked David, who was driving, to stop so he could say hello to the neighbors he had known for years. In the car, we had asked Clive what Richard and Alisa's story was. He said Richard was an old Etonian and he believed Alisa had some connection to the queen.

When we arrived, David waited outside the door.

"Aren't you coming in?" I asked. He said no, that the people in his village didn't get on with Richard.

I looked at the entrance to the house, which had a beautifully lettered, soaring quote by Nobel laureate Rigoberta Menchú Tum, a Mayan human rights activist: "We are not myths of the past, ruins in the jungle, or zoos. We are Maya people and we want to be respected . . ."

I looked at David. He shrugged as if to say it wasn't uncommon for people to venerate an idea more than their actual living neighbors.

Sarka waited in the car. She has trypophobia—a fear or aversion to irregular patterns or clusters of small holes or bumps—which is a highly accurate description of the Earthship that Alisa had named Chaos Oasis.

After Moody and I moved in at Fallen Stones, we didn't visit the oasis often because of tensions between Richard and Sebastian, our Mayan host. But we figured Kat and Jed's visit gave us an excuse, and I was fascinated by our British neighbors. They were both lean, beautiful creatures in what I guessed was their forties. Both seemed slightly mad, or perhaps madcap, about a slew of things from organic herb gardens to macabre true-crime shows to their three children who were scattered about the globe studying interesting things.

"I wonder how they got the name Chaos Oasis," Moody asked as we arrived with Kat and Jed. "Is it an oasis away from chaos or an oasis of chaos?"

Kat studied the Earthship with almost as much intensity as she had when she'd watched the butterflies. Jed particularly liked the Chaos Oasis bar where a huge glass mosaic crystal skull gazed from the wall. Recessed shelves held several bottles of Crystal Head vodka, a Canadian brand founded by Dan Aykroyd that comes in a skull-shaped bottle. Alisa had written the former Blues Brother several times, hoping for a case of skulls, but had yet to receive a reply. If you're ever traveling to Southern Belize, you should bring them a bottle.

The reason for the theme was that a crystal skull had been unearthed at Lubaantun by Anna Mitchell-Hedges in 1924 or 1926 (she gave various dates). Mitchell-Hedges was the daughter of expedition leader F. A. Mitchell-Hedges, who later became the podcaster of his time, with a popular Sunday-evening radio show. Over the sound of jungle drums, he recounted supposed adventures he'd had in far-away lands, such as being attacked by a vicious iguana.

Modern technology had since revealed his expedition's discovery at Lubaantun to be a scam, a bamboozle. The crystal skull was a fake. Or was it?

The international crystal skull societies, who sometimes gathered at Lubaantun, believed it was real. They believed it to be a cosmic portal.

Alisa was a wonderful storyteller. She had the presence of the stage actress that she had once been. But her stories came so fast and furiously that they made my head spin.

The day that she first told me of the crystal skull, I lost track of the various plot twists. I only gathered that she believed the crystal skull was real, held some kind of power, and that a friend of theirs kept the talisman—the actual skull from the story—at a karate studio in Indiana. I made a mental note to ask her to explain the details later.

On earlier visits, Richard had not been as effusive as Alisa. But on the day we visited with Kat and Jed, he and Jed hit it off over their mutual interest in making colloidal silver, an undertaking apparently involving a car battery and the family silver.

Richard had, on an earlier visit, given me a small blue bottle of it when I'd complained about mosquito bites. The label read: "Use on cuts, bites and stings, acne and conjunctivitis, diaper rash, burns and heat rash. Safe and effective on the whole family even pets!"

I cannot speak to the other ailments, but, alas, like everything else, it proved useless on mosquito bites.

The visit was a success. Even Moody, who is not the most social of butterflies, liked shooting the breeze with Richard about the latest crime stories in the local paper and world politics. Richard said they should smoke cigars sometime. Moody agreed, even though he didn't smoke—that I knew about.

That evening, back at the house, the bats all left at a reasonable hour. A breeze kept the mosquitoes at bay. Kat offered to make dinner and produced rice bowls that were as colorful as the Chaos Oasis, Jed's piled high with a profusion of poultry.

Moody had told Kat that the butterfly farm was remote and quiet. She had said that was perfect. She needed some rest from her job managing the only market for miles in a rural area.

But it had been a few days of relative seclusion, and we were planning to ask them if they wanted to go snorkeling in the cays or take a boat ride through crocodile-infested waters or go on any of Belize's other storied adventures during the rest of their visit.

We didn't get a chance. Jed took the conversational reins. He told us that his parents were hippies. *Real* hippies, he emphasized. He reported his lineage with the smugness of someone announcing they were third-generation Harvard. In both cases, I wasn't sure how the progeny got the credit.

His parents met during a game of nude volleyball on the beach in Mexico. So perhaps a willingness to spike unclothed was what elevated them in authenticity.

When his real-hippie father lived in Santa Cruz, California, he had a best friend from Guatemala. He hadn't seen him in thirty years. Jed's father was aging and had early signs of Alzheimer's. Jed was going to find the Guatemalan friend for him and take photos, maybe FaceTime. I thought this sounded soulful and caring.

Then he said that he and Kat would be taking the ferry to Guatemala the next day to look for the friend.

No, he didn't have an address.

No, his family hadn't had any contact with this man for thirty years.

Moody stared. I stared. They were returning to California in five days.

Jed seemed to think we should find his endeavor noble. Kat did.

She patted Jed's arm and said in a proud, respectful hush, "It's im-por-taint."

Jed slowly noticed we were not gushing over his quest.

"I looked at a map, and Guatemala was right there. What are you going to do?" he asked.

"Well," growled Moody, "what you could do is go to Guatemala and leave my daughter here."

"It's no big deal," said Jed. "There's nothing to be upset about."

There are few things worse than watching someone you love get hurt. Unless it's watching someone you love get hurt and then trying not to show it so his besotted daughter won't see. I was appalled.

Then I was mad that Jed had turned me into a pearl-clutching matron thinking things like, *I am appalled.*

The next morning, we had to get up early to take Jed and Kat to the ferry in PG. Jed said it left at 9:30.

I was looking at the bright side—we could stick them on the boat, which at this point, I was more than ready to do, then go have a Belizean breakfast of eggs, black beans, fry jack, and fresh pineapple juice.

But at the ferry, the schedule sign said the boat left at 11:30. I was beginning to see how they may have missed their plane.

Jed went to get tickets. Moody went to talk to John, who owned our favorite market in PG. We'd been reading about an outbreak of a strange new virus in Wuhan, and John was originally from China. Moody wanted to see if John's family was okay.

Kat and I were left alone in the car.

"Hey," I ventured. "Was this something Jed sprang on you? Or did you know all along?"

There was an icy silence.

I backpedaled. I'd known Kat since she was nine, and we'd always had an open, friendly relationship, but maybe things were different now that I was with her father.

"Probably none of my business," I said.

"It's all good," said Kat, using that popular phrase of total dismissal. "We're all people," she added.

We're all people—how could one argue with such a universal truth?

Moody returned with news from John; he'd heard about the virus, but his family was safe—they lived several hours from Wuhan. We still had an hour to wait, and it was Belize hot. Moody and I sat in the car while Jed and Kat bought fried-fish burritos from a questionable-looking shack before the ferry ride.

"Shall we leave them to catch their boat and go to breakfast?" I suggested.

"I don't want to miss any time with my daughter," Moody said.

"But she is out there, and we are in here," I observed.

"I can see her," he said, watching the lovely Kat through the windshield.

When it was time for the ferry to take them across the Bay of Honduras to Livingston, where the friend who hadn't been seen in thirty years supposedly lived, I hollered to Kat that she had left her backpack in the car.

"Only need my toothbrush," she said, showing it in her pocket. So why then had they packed up and put everything in the Jeep? Supposedly, they were coming back tomorrow or the next day.

Over the next few days, Moody would sigh deeply and, apropos of nothing, say things such as, "You're supposed to do your own thing when you're young." Or suddenly he'd recall that he'd seldom phoned his parents when he was traveling the world.

I thought of a trip to Tahoe with a boyfriend's family. His parents had paid for everything, and we'd spent as much time alone as possible. I'm so sorry, Mr. and Mrs. Parks.

Of course, Jed found the friend right away. When he said he was going to Guatemala to find a guy whose address he didn't know, Jed had failed to mention that the man is Garifuna. The Garifuna are the descendants of never-enslaved Africans who mixed with Caribs. Their ancestors were on a ship from Nigeria that wrecked before reaching the Americas. They are a distinct, tight-knit community with their own Afro-Caribbean music, language, and food.

Livingston is a small Garifuna town on the mouth of the Rio Dulce and a bay in Honduras, and you can only get there by boat. It was the kind of place where Jed only had to ask a couple of people to find the right house.

The dad's friend was ecstatic to see Jed and Kat. They partied and went to waterfalls. How can you compete with that? Kat texted to see if we wanted to go snorkeling the day before we took them to the airport.

Alli said she could arrange a boat. I told Alli to wait until we knew for sure Kat and Jed were on that ferry.

Alli was in a happy mood. She had closed Hickatee for three days and was taking time off for the first time in four months. I kidded her, asking how many rooms she would be painting in her downtime. It was odd how, wherever I went, the universe gave me a highly industrious friend. It was like I was supposed to be inspired to hop to it.

We waited for a text from Kat saying they were on the boat. Instead, I got a girlfriend-to-girlfriend call from Alli.

She had closed up her hotel for her break. Locked the big, tall gates. Let loose their two dogs onto the grounds. They were not meant to be friendly dogs to anyone but her family. These dogs' job was protection.

In the meantime, Jed and Kat had only been able to get the night ferry and came in the evening before we were supposed to meet them. Kat's phone was dead. Jed had not paid the twenty dollars to make his phone work in Belize.

They took a cab to Hickatee, three miles west of town. When they found the six-foot gate locked, Jed climbed over. The dogs went ballistic, frightening Alli and her sons but not Jed. Alli's security system was cast in doubt.

Alli lowered her voice to tell me that Jed had reeked of alcohol and Kat had twisted her ankle. I was glad I hadn't booked a snorkeling boat.

I confessed I had mixed feelings about the dogs not cornering Jed.

"It's not like you would want him bit," said Alli. "But a little scared wouldn't have been bad."

Alli put them up, despite being on a much-needed break, and added their stay to the tab we were running for sending our laundry down and getting grocery deliveries. It was the last of Alli's two nights off during the dry season. I added mortified to appalled on my list of new reactions and grew more distant from my youth.

Instead of going to meet the ferry, Moody and I began readying to go to Hickatee so we could take Jed and Kat to lunch, since Kat couldn't walk and we didn't want Alli to have to open her kitchen.

I began brushing my teeth and grew angry. It wasn't the first time brushing my teeth had led me to a fit. Think about it: brushing your teeth properly takes a solid two minutes with nothing to do but stew, and on top of that, you're kind of already making a sneer and shaking your fist.

I returned from the bathroom with minty fresh breath and a bunch of "whos":

"*Who* goes to a small hotel in a remote jungle area at night without calling? *Who* takes his girlfriend away from time visiting her dad in order to set up a video chat with his dad's long-lost pal? *Who* doesn't tell her dad the *real* plan is *Guatemala*?"

Moody was taken aback, not yet being familiar with my connection between oral hygiene and sudden irateness.

"Listen," he said. "Because your parents died when you were a teenager, you were never really twenty. Being clueless is the point of your twenties. I was a total fuckup at that age."

"This runs in the family?" I gasped.

But he was right, in a way. We all hold previous versions of ourselves, and inside me was a daughter who would have given anything for more time with her dad. She was the one who was mad. Present-day me should lighten up.

A quirk of scheduling meant that my friend Alice, a news director for a radio station back home, was arriving for a visit the day before Jed and Kat left.

We'd booked everyone rooms at Hickatee, talked Alli into joining the party, and had a buffet dinner delivered from a restaurant. Alli, with a twinkle, said that she couldn't figure out a way to seat us all together, so she asked if it would be alright if Moody sat with Jed and Kat, her sons had a kids' table, and she and I and Alice had a grown-up women's table.

At the grown-up women's table, Alli served her trademark cocktail, pink Gin-Gins.

After I quickly recounted my day, Alice suggested I consider buying an electric toothbrush. Alli suggested another Gin-Gin. By the time Jed came over to show us the photos of the spectacular waterfall, I was ready to genuinely admire them. I was even ready to concede that Jed meant well.

I recently asked for Alli's Gin-Gin recipe. Here is what she sent, verbatim:

Alli's Gin-Gins
Half lime squeezed (Jamaican lime is my fav)
2 oz. (2.5 oz. for me) dry gin—Tanqueray preferred
Ice to chill the gin
Top with ginger ale (my fav is ginger beer for an added punch)
Splash of grenadine to make it pretty

Must drink two in a sitting to fully enjoy.

In the morning, I begged off the drive to take Kat and Jed to the airport because I had Alice visiting and there wasn't room for everyone in the Jeep. When Moody returned to our room at Hickatee, he said that Jed had given him gifts upon leaving.

"Really?" I asked.

"Oh, yes," said Moody. "Look."

He'd given Moody a feather to give to Profilio, who had guided them to the waterfall one afternoon.

Jed had duct-taped the feather to the underside brim of a teal-green trucker's hat, and it stuck out on both sides.

Moody said Jed had seemed to hesitate as he was handing over the hat, but then said mostly to himself, "I never *really* liked that hat."

He had also given Moody a bottle of duty-free Crystal Head vodka to give to Richard.

It was half gone.

Moody and I locked eyes in a dare to see who would laugh first. I think it was a tie.

On the way back to Fallen Stones, we stopped in PG for produce. As Alice and I picked out pineapples, I wondered if Moody was right, and Jed and Kat were simply young—human instars who could evolve soon into a slightly different form. Maybe Kat would move to a stage where she needed a more reflective surface for her love. Maybe each of them would spin a chrysalis and emerge ready for dazzling flight.

Moody was getting sunburned and went back to the Jeep for his hat. He couldn't find it, grabbed the one meant for Profilio, and stomped around the market with a feather sticking out both sides of his head.

Eleven

Alice

We left Hickatee and arrived at Fallen Stones with Alice just before sunset. The sky was bright blue and the clouds were dollops of fluffed cream.

Alice literally gasped at the view. I felt like when you foist a favorite book on a friend and they love it too. Within minutes, as if there were an opening curtain, the colors changed to rose pinks and tangerines.

Moody and I tried to explain to Alice which of the many sounds were the toucans.

"The one that's like a frog: crk-crk-crk," Moody said.

"But a different rhythm," I said. "More like, crk-crk crk-crk-crk."

Despite our help, Alice was able to figure it out.

Alice was my adventuring friend who had set me on roads I might not have otherwise traveled.

As the youngest of six children, she'd been left mostly free to run around the woods of Tennessee until her zoologist father moved the family to Kenya in her teens. Her parents had once crammed the whole regiment into a rented car and drove around Europe over spring break. Alice liked to travel to far-off lands and do things like ski straight down mountains.

I, on the other hand, had been raised in a family where people said things such as, "Can you believe those crazy people strapping sticks on their feet and hurtling down a mountain? You won't catch me doing that!"

My family's idea of travel was a yearly drive to Oregon to check in with kin and hear accounts of any births, deaths, or surgeries. We always began the journey well before dawn, my brother and I still in pajamas, so as to make the drive in one day. (Although we did once spend the night at a KOA camp, that holy temple of budget family fun, and that was very exciting.)

Moody, an excellent skier, insinuates I overuse "I grew up poor" as self-explanation. But I think a person soaks up the caution of a family living paycheck to paycheck, always fearing unexpected blows. Poor people don't ski—what if something happens and you can't go to work?

When Alice and I first became friends, I was a new staff writer at the local paper in Fresno and she was teaching journalism part-time at the college. I wasn't rolling in dough, but I was single, without real financial responsibilities. I had my fingernails on the ledge to lower middle class because I'd inherited the product of my parents' endless hopes and sacrifices.

A mutual friend, Selena, was going to Paris to run a marathon and heal a broken heart. The three of us sat at our local French bakery downing croissants and discussing the trip. I was starry-eyed at Selena's plan.

"Why don't you go too?" Alice asked.

I laughed. Yeah, right. Why didn't I grow feathers and fly there? I was hardly the sort of person who just picked up and went to Paris.

"Seriously," said Alice. "Airfare is cheap right now. You have a job. Put it on a credit card."

I didn't have a credit card.

"I'll loan you the money," said Alice, immediately writing a check.

It only took two paychecks, after paying bills, to repay Alice for the plane ticket. Mostly I gave up our local French bakery for a bit to save the money. The trip was a revelation. It had been possible to do things like that all along, and I'd never realized it. That's one of the bonus costs of poverty on top of its more insidious hardships—even if you do climb out, it can leave you a little nearsighted, not privy to all that is out there and with a stunted view of your ability to partake.

In Paris, a breakfast of fresh croissants, orange juice, and a bowl of coffee was included in the price of my modest room beneath a slanted roof in a Notre-Dame neighborhood. For lunch, I went each day to a Lebanese place frequented by immigrants and had a five-euro falafel with salad and rice. This left me enough funds for a pistachio gelato for dinner. For entertainment, I simply walked around eating my ice cream. It was the only thing I could afford and the most perfect thing I could do.

After that Alice-spurred trip, I thought of myself as the kind of person who might just pick up and go to Paris. And the kind of person who might do a lot of other things, such as move to Belize and live on a butterfly farm. So it seemed really fitting that she had come to visit.

That first night, Alice and I were standing on the balcony when we saw a bright flash of light that disappeared as quickly as it had come.

It seemed to be coming from up top.

"It's the moon," said Moody when we told him about it.

"No, it was *really* bright," I said.

"And it disappeared," added Alice.

Alice and I decided we would investigate. Climbing to the top at night still gave me a little bit of the shivers—you could feel eyes watching, and they didn't all belong to spiders. Alice charged up the stones, and I carefully picked my footsteps behind her.

The entire way, there were flashes of bright light and then darkness. We couldn't see where the light was coming from.

Sometimes it can be fun to incite a sliver of inner superstition. The closer we got to the top, the closer we got to Lubaantun.

Actually, strike that, Lubaantun's boundaries were modern day, in no way tied to the ancient Maya. The most recent research showed that the whole area, really the entirety of Belize, was part of the Mayan Empire. We were already walking on top of ruins.

The week before, Profilio had told me that when he was a child, he and his best friend used to set off from the village to Lubaantun.

"Like Tom Sawyer and Huckleberry Finn," he had said, which made me smile. San Pedro's Columbia River was a long way from the Mississippi, but the imagery of two young adventurers was spot on.

He said they would go on Sunday when they had the place to themselves. The two boys would wander the hills and hide in the shade of the cohune palms, and Profilio could hear a whispering the whole expedition. He felt his ancestors were talking to him.

I had asked if he meant human ancestors in general or his ancestors in particular, given the belief that San Pedro Columbia was settled in the late 1800s by refugees from Guatemala.

He said it was his particular ancestors. His theory was that no one knew what happened to the people who had disappeared from Lubaantun all those centuries ago. Who was to say they hadn't fled from whatever drove them out and went to the mountains in what is now Guatemala? Then generations and generations later, when they were on the run, something deep inside called them to the Columbia River and these verdant foothills. Something called them home.

This gave my imagination plenty to work with as Alice and I climbed toward the flashing light on top of the hill. Were ghosts of ancient ancestors having a bonfire? Would we hear whispers from another world?

In a way, we did. When we crested the hill, we saw the moon. It hung huge and low and was partially covered by long streams of clouds. As we watched, the streams separated like blinds pushed open, and the full moon was a floodlight on our plateau.

On the way back, I considered telling Moody in jest that we'd surprised drug runners or seen ghosts, but that moon seemed a spectacular enough tale to carry home.

In order to get time away from her radio station without using vacation days, Alice had pitched a story: "Local Writer Moves to Butterfly Farm." The next day, with her headphones and boom mike, she visited the farm.

Even when Alice isn't working, she asks more questions than anyone I've ever met. I have to clamp my mouth shut and not be enticed by her attentions in order to ever find out anything about her.

I trailed after her as she plastered Profilio, Nestor, and Sebastian with her unwavering curiosity.

She probably found out in two hours as much about the inner workings of raising butterflies as I had learned in two months. But the joke was on her. She'd have to cut that tape down to two minutes.

She had plenty of off-the-record questions too. The main one, which Moody and I both struggled to answer: How exactly had we been spending our time?

"You know," said Moody, "it's kind of hard to say."

There was nothing specific to point to. Books had gone unread. Art supplies unused. The whining inverter gave us enough phone charge to get news of the world but in finite amounts. It was like the days when there was a print paper.

All I knew was that the greatest luxury in life is to wake up and unhurriedly think, *Hmm, what do I want to learn about today?* But it was a time-consuming gift.

On the third day of Alice's four-day visit, we grew ambitious and left the butterfly farm early in the morning to head for the sea.

We were going out with Captain Neville, a taut, opinionated man who bounced each of his steps and always wore reflective shades and a wide smile. Captain Neville oozed cocky swagger. This was good. There are some professions such as surgeons, boat captains, and fire dancers that require self-assuredness.

Most of the captains in the area were for hire on boats owned by companies or NGOs. Captain Neville owned his boat. His single mother, a schoolteacher, had risked her life savings to help him buy it. He had told his mother that he wasn't going to let her or his own daughters down. He had grown up in the area, and he planned on being a force in Toledo tourism. Toledo wasn't on most tourist itineraries; it got about 2 percent of foreign travelers who weren't already on cruise-ship tours or staying at a fishing lodge. But Captain Neville would be ready to take those independent tourists out on the water.

It felt good to be on the ocean again, something familiar to me. The butterfly farm in the jungle was a foreign world, endlessly fascinating but daunting too. On the boat, the wind whipped in my face, and I breathed cool, salty air as we sped to the coast guard station at Abalone Caye. Alice's brown hair was cut in a bob that held its lines even when whipping around. Back home, we had the same hairstylist. I idly wondered when I'd have a hairstyle again and pulled my baseball cap tighter to clamp down the frizz.

Everyone—tourist or local—going into the Port Honduras Marine Reserve was required to stop at the coast guard station first. When we docked, an old, gray-muzzled brown dog came wiggling down, greeting Captain Neville.

We were led into a room to hear a presentation on gill net fishing. The gill nets, some a mile long, indiscriminately caught everything: sea turtles, coral, threatened species, and sports fish with supposed catch limits. Inside the marine sanctuaries, the nets were illegal, and the coast guard patrolled, arresting those who used them in protected waters.

Captain Neville walked outside as the slideshow played. I figured he must have heard the presentation a dozen times.

Our fees paid, the coast guard's mission digested, we motored out into the most beautiful ocean setting I have ever seen. That is a dangerous statement for me to write. I'm a Californian. I spent a year in the Azores. I feel claims of disloyalty gathering.

But in terms of "jump in and play," it would be hard to top the Caribbean Sea on that day. Looking out and across, the water was flat and smooth, a pale blue inlaid with bright turquoise. Looking down, it was clear.

We needed no wet suits. To enter a different universe, we only had to stick some scuba fins on our feet and put our faces under the water.

At first, I only saw coral. There were rounded ones that looked like human brains (and were indeed called brain coral), ruffle-edged lettuce corals, and branching corals that looked like fluorescent flower gardens under black lights.

But soon, I noticed there were as many fish as in the window of an aquarium. Schools of navy-gray chubs and parrotfish—bright blue, rainbow colored, yellow, and striped—fluttered past. How could I not compare them to butterflies? A huge old lobster walked stiffly around like a battery-operated toy, and crabs scuttled along the sand and gravel bottom. The display was a fraction of the sights that waited forty miles farther out, on the reef, but was enough to dazzle me.

The silence beneath the water was all-encompassing. I could only hear my own heartbeat and breathing.

Hours later, we climbed up on the boat for a lunch of curried vegetables and rice from one of the local East Indian restaurants. There was an East Indian community in Toledo that traced back to when their ancestors arrived as indentured servants to work the sugar plantations, a thinly veiled work-around after slavery had been outlawed. Some families also arrived in 1858, after the British government brutally suppressed an uprising. One thousand Indian independence fighters were deported, with their wives and families, to Belize. It wasn't the first time I'd notice how much history could be found in one meal.

I brought up the subject of gill nets. Neville said he used to be a member of the coast guard. No wonder the dog had known him.

One night, he came upon a small boat with a long, mostly empty gill net. He shone his searchlight on the boat. There was one man and his son. The boy looked to be about eight years old. It was a chilly night, and he had been curled up asleep under a net.

"He didn't even have a blanket," Neville said. The man looked terrified and put up his hands. He was Guatemalan and only spoke Spanish, a language Neville didn't speak.

He was supposed to arrest the man and confiscate his boat and equipment. Instead, he confiscated only the net and hoped the father and son made it home safely. The next day, he quit the coast guard.

"How is it right to arrest people who are starving when the government still lets big guys net?" he asked. "I want no part of that." (In November 2020, Belize banned gill nets after a twenty-year push by environmentalists, the association of small fisherman, and local communities.)

Neville was trying to protect the waters where he grew up fishing and diving in his own way. Plastic bottles and trash washed up in piles on the mangroves and the small, uninhabited cays. On weekends when he didn't have paying tourists, he took local kids who would normally not get to go on the ocean, to pick up the litter. The soccer team from San Pedro Columbia was scheduled that weekend.

I liked Neville's DIY version of cleaning the environment and opening horizons for kids. It was good to be reminded that you don't have to be a millionaire like Clive or a Rothschild to get things going.

After lunch, Neville said he'd take us to a good swimming spot. I was thinking I was probably swum out, and Alice and Moody were both napping.

But when Captain Neville cut the engines—well, you know how I said earlier that it was the most beautiful ocean scene I had ever seen? Our new surroundings upped the ante. There was a thin, deserted cay with the requisite palms. The white sand of the beach extended all the way out to the boat, covered with about five feet of clear turquoise water.

I floated on my back looking at the sky. I hoped I could recall this feeling of freedom and ease when I needed to.

Weeks later, after Alice was back home and ensconced in her work-aday life, I wrote and asked if the beautiful things in Belize did stick and carry once a person was back in their normal routine.

"Yes," she wrote back. "The trees and birds and butterflies carry, although they get put in the stream with the detritus so you have to be careful not to lose sight of them."

Twelve

Scorpions

We didn't mean to stack our visitors up like layers in a Neapolitan pastry. The idea, after all, was for me to focus on the farm. But Alice was barely out the door when it was time for Jordan to visit on one of the only weekends she had free.

Jordan had been ready to fly from Miami, bag and seal mattresses, scrub down walls, and retile the shower, back when she thought I'd be living like a Navy SEAL. So it was very nice to invite her for a weekend stay, smooth the linen sheets on her bed, and put fresh jungle foliage in a vase to ready her room.

When Jordan stepped off the plane, I noticed a few things: She was limping. She had one arm in a sling and her wrist in a brace, and she was carrying duty-free gin.

I hoped the last item wasn't all she had for pain relief: it was 159 steep, irregularly spaced stones from the parking spot to the house. Jordan had seen the photos.

I gave her a hug, then looked at her with raised eyebrows.

She laughed.

"Skiing accident. I didn't tell you because I knew you'd worry, Marcum," she said.

(My suspicions about skiing, validated once again.)

It was sunset and we were headed straight to Fallen Stones. For someone who traveled as much as Jordan did, Miami to Belize was a quick popover.

Moody stopped at a large gas station outside PG to fill up the Jeep. It was off the highway in a big asphalt parking lot.

Still, we heard them as soon as we opened the doors. This time, it wasn't the whomp-whomp of howler monkeys in the distance: it was the loud, unworldly roar of howler monkeys just across an empty lot.

I had spent months, to no avail, hoping to glimpse the howlers at the remote, lush butterfly sanctuary. We hadn't even heard them in the distance, and their voices can carry three miles. Yet here they were plain as day at a gas station.

We stood beside a trash dumpster and watched the biggest of the Central American monkeys moving around the trees using their tails like another arm. They were so loud that we could barely hear one another over the din.

"Welcome to Belize, Jordan," Moody shouted. "Wait until you see what comes with an oil change."

Over dinner on our balcony, with a background chorus of katydids and crickets, we got caught up. In late January, Jordan had sent me a snapshot of her skiing with friends at the highest ski resort in Europe. She had looked happy but cold, and it amused me that we were sharing images between Belizean rain forest and the French Alps. She'd taken a bad tumble. She kept skiing but had injured her wrist and shoulder.

Right after she got home, she came down with the worst flu of her life. She was bedridden for more than a week, making her injuries an afterthought.

"That bug knocked me out so badly. I don't think I've ever been that sick," she said.

In the morning, Jordan drank coffee and chatted with Marcellinus, Sebastian's brother, as he passed the house with his leaves. He always cut and carried the biggest bundles.

Jordan limped down with us to the butterfly farm to contribute a bag of banana peels and lime pieces for Anselmo and Julio to put on plates at the blue morphos' fruit bar.

When the temperature rose, we walked back to the house and the afternoon lull settled. Moody stretched out for a nap. I opened a mystery book set in snowy Canada. Jordan was taking a shower in her room.

So I was surprised to hear her announce herself outside our open bedroom door. "Knock. Knock."

Her voice sounded odd. A strangled stage whisper.

Jordan then appeared, swathed in one white towel with a towering towel turban on her head. Her aquamarine eyes stood out against her forever-Florida-tan, pops of unmistakable anxiety.

"You guys. I don't want to alarm you," she said in the overly measured voice of someone who is clearly freaking out. "But there is a scorpion in my shower."

We were not alarmed.

Moody nodded.

"Oh, okay," he said.

"We have two scorpions that live in the kitchen," I said. "Above the oatmeal. But they only come out at night."

I lumped them in with the occasional tarantula on the deck, the bats on the wall, and the semi-regular invasion of ants in the shower. And I always looked very carefully before moving the oatmeal.

"You guys," said Jordan in a sharp pay-attention tone. "I don't think you understand. Scorpions are deadly."

She told us that she had done survival training in Libya. (I loved Jordan's endless biographical surprises. Alice was my fun adventurer friend. Jordan was my "what exactly did you once do for a living?" friend.) During the training, she had spent two days on simulations involving scorpions with a fast-acting venom.

"Oh," said Moody. "Would you like me to move it?"

"We'll have to be very careful," Jordan said, thoughtfully nodding her towering head towel.

She and Moody began strategic planning. They seemed to have it well under control, and I was at a good part of my novel, so I read a few more pages until I heard Moody downstairs in the kitchen clattering among our limited cookware.

He appeared with a pot and lid.

"Hold on there, cowboy," I said (surprising myself, because I didn't know I was given to saying "Hold on there, cowboy"). "That's our only pasta pot."

"There's nothing else," he said like an Apollo astronaut ready to fashion an air-filtration canister from cardboard and masking tape.

"Moody, I'm not sure this is safe," I said as he marched into Jordan's room. I felt distressed, although my foremost worry was still scorpion cooties on the only thing we had in which to cook spaghetti.

Jordan touched my arm and whispered to me with grave, sisterly concern. "Don't try to stop him. You'll insult his masculinity."

I went back to my book. A few minutes later, Moody returned and reported that he had enclosed the scorpion by clamping the pot on the wall. He then used a thin plastic cutting board to slide between the pot and the wall, knocking the scorpion into the pot. He plopped on the lid and carried the scorpion outside, far from Jordan's shower.

Jordan, now fully dressed and combed, appeared in our doorway.

"I just wanted to thank Moody and let both of you know that if things had gone wrong, I had a plan," she said. "I wouldn't want you to worry."

"A plan?" we asked in unison.

"In case Moody got stung," Jordan clarified.

We both put down our books.

"What was your plan if I got bit?" six-foot Moody asked five-foot-two Jordan, who now had her wrist brace and shoulder sling back on.

"I was going to hoist you in a fireman's carry and get you up to the Jeep," she said. "If the key wasn't in the ignition, I could have gotten the Jeep rolling down the hill and popped the clutch. I noticed an umbrella in your back seat," she added. "If I couldn't reach the clutch with my bad leg, I was going to use the umbrella."

"You have an injured shoulder," Moody said.

"I was going to throw you over the *other* shoulder," Jordan said.

"It's a hundred and fifty-nine stairs," said Moody. He was careful to keep a straight face, but the bed was shaking with suppressed laughter.

"Hey, wait a minute," I said, chiming in. "It was going to hurt Moody's masculine sense of pride for me to ask him to not use the pasta pot, but it's okay for you to toss him over your good shoulder?"

"Well, he'd be unconscious," said Jordan.

"And what would I be doing, carrying your purse?" I asked. I, too, was deadpan, but tears were forming from the effort.

"You can never count on how a person is going to behave in an emergency," Jordan told me. "You could have freaked. You may have fainted."

"I would not have fainted!" I exclaimed, genuinely affronted that in a scenario where a venomous scorpion rendered Moody unconscious and Jordan flung him over her good shoulder and trekked up 159 stone steps, I was to be relegated to a swooning heap.

"Well, what would *you* have done?" Jordan asked defensively.

"I would have texted Sebastian," I said with a shrug.

"Aha!" Jordan leapt on my faulty planning. "The. Cell. Signal. Does. *Not*. Work at the butterfly cages."

Which is exactly why it would be extremely likely that one of the workers would be near the house texting someone when the scorpion crawled out of the spaghetti pot and got Moody, I thought.

But then I saw a more impressive wilderness-survival answer. Two stout branches were propped against the wall. It was how two men had carried down our propane refrigerator.

"I'd have made a litter with those sticks," I said.

Jordan examined the sticks. "That could work," she said appraisingly.

"Works like a charm with major appliances," I said. "You and I could have run him up in no time. Or if you had freaked out and tore off into the woods in a blind panic, I could have used the hammock and dragged him up," I added as payback for the dead faint she had ascribed to me.

"Well, great to know I'm in good hands," said Moody. "But once you got to the Jeep, where exactly were you going to take me?" he asked. "Also, the Jeep is an automatic. It doesn't have a clutch." It seemed like a good thing neither of us had to spring into action.

Crises averted and future calamities partially prepared for, we went to meet Profilio for a hike to the waterfall.

To me, the whole sanctuary was jungle. But to Sebastian and others old enough to remember what it had looked like before the fire, the only real jungle left was around the trails near the waterfall. By the farm, the vegetation was vines and slender trees. Here, the great buttresses of mahogany trees still plowed up the earth, and above them, vines twisted and dangled hundreds of feet down from thick, heavy branches.

Sebastian preferred that we had a guide when we hiked this part of the property. It wasn't a hard-and-fast rule. Early on in our stay, Moody had walked to the waterfall alone with Sebastian's blessing.

When Moody returned, he had told me, "I wouldn't say it was scary, but, yeah, I probably don't need to do that again."

Which meant it was scary.

With Jordan, Sebastian had asked Profilio to guide us. It was Profilio's dream to save up the one thousand Belizean dollars the government charged to take the tests required to become an official tour guide. Clive paid more than the Belizean minimum wage of $3.30. But even if Profilio made $6, that fee would be a lot of money to squirrel away while supporting his family. If he pulled it off, it would be a gift to anyone who experienced nature in his company. Few could marvel at the natural world as contagiously as Profilio.

We found him cutting weeds next to an old, abandoned flight house that was full of spiderwebs and spiders. It had been abandoned because ants had invaded, eating butterfly eggs and caterpillars. Then the spiders came to eat the ants. The newer butterfly houses were all on short stilts set in pools of water so the ants couldn't cross their moats—just like the one that housed Sammy's butterflies.

When we stopped in, I told Profilio about our scorpion debacle, thinking he would get a laugh at our idiocy. He glanced sharply at Moody.

"You carried it out alive?" he said.

"Of course," said Moody. "You trained me well, Profilio. I wouldn't kill anything here."

"Did it look like the big scorpions living in your kitchen?"

"It was smaller," said Moody. "And kind of misshapen."

Profilio looked green.

"Where did you put it?" he said.

Moody pointed vaguely to the field. "Why? Profilio, what's wrong?" he asked.

Profilio could sometimes be as indirect as Sebastian. First, he began with the state of the planet.

"The animals in the jungle are very mystical," he said. "Some people take from the jungle and they don't care. Everything is going to extinction. It's one thing to see it in books, but to see these creatures alive . . . ," he said.

The three of us nodded in agreement.

Profilio still looked green.

"The scorpion is a king. They are magnificent. They are rulers. But you don't touch that poison. It can cripple you with double, triple, the pain. It can disable you. I once was stung by the king, and my circulation stopped."

(I learned later that scorpions in Belize are generally not deadly but can cause heart arrhythmia.)

"Thank God," I said, "that it was only one small scorpion."

"The smaller ones are the most dangerous. Also, this is the time when lady scorpions have babies," Profilio said. "The babies are born alive, and she may have a hundred of them."

Moody looked closely at the spider-filled flight house.

"Do scorpions eat spiders?" he asked.

"Yes," Profilio said. "And ants. Let us be walking."

It was a fun walk, even if the first part took us past potentially thousands of scorpion babies. We saw a palm with a frond growing in a circle, so we took turns sticking our faces through the open middle like we were posing with a photo cutout board of a lion's mane at an amusement park. Profilio grabbed a giant dried seedpod from a cohune tree. It was about three feet long and curved like a shallow bowl. He showed us how he and his friends used to drag each other in them like sleds. I spotted a brilliant-orange bug on a bright-green leaf, and there were the spiky orange cones of bromeliads growing on the side of trees.

A huge vine as thick as a fist grew across the trail. We had to duck beneath it.

"Water vine," said Profilio. "It starts small, and you can't tell by looking at it, but in a disaster in the forest, it's your major support."

He said that if he cut it with his machete, drinking water would pour out.

If that wasn't already enough nature knowledge that could be taken as metaphor, Jordan asked him how it was possible to navigate the untouched jungle in the valleys and mountains around Fallen Stones.

"If you get lost, you must find a river and follow its flow," Profilio said. "But you must observe carefully and make sure it's the right river." The trail narrowed and we walked single file. I was behind Profilio. He turned and put a finger to his lips. I walked forward very quietly to see what treasure he had spotted this time.

Here is the embarrassing part: I ran. As soon as I gathered what was in front of us, I ran away quickly and blindly and, for the first time since I'd been in Belize, did not pay attention to where I was stepping.

The interesting part is that I never really saw the snake. Or else my phobia immediately blotted it from my consciousness, finding the sight of it too much to take. I ran without my mind *seeing* a snake. I have no image of it in my mind now.

Moody described it to me later. It was yellow. About five feet long. Head high in the tree, within arm's reach of the trail, wound around several branches. Profilio said it wasn't poisonous. Moody said he'd never seen anything like it. Jordan took a photo that she later offered to show me. I declined.

Profilio was the first to catch up to me.

"I'm sorry!" we both said at the same time.

"I didn't know," he said.

"I didn't tell you," I said. "It's so stupid. A few times now, I thought I saw something slither by and got sick to my stomach. But this time, I just ran before I even knew I was running. It makes no sense. I have no history with snakes," I said.

Maybe it was something I recalled from my caterpillar days when I was just the building blocks of what someday became me.

In 2007, scientists at Georgetown discovered memories could be retained through metamorphosis. The scientists, Martha R. Weiss, Douglas J. Blackiston, and Elena Silva Casey, trained tobacco hornworm caterpillars to avoid the odor of ethyl acetate (the chemical that gives nail polish the bad smell). Caterpillars are usually indifferent to the scent, but the researchers paired it with mild electric shocks, and 78 percent of the caterpillars learned to avoid the smell.

The caterpillars went into their pupal case to turn into moths. Metamorphosis begins with a process called histolysis. Enzymes dissolve a caterpillar into liquid, a soup of proteins. Then a group of specialized cells called histoblasts use that goo to reconstruct a butterfly or a moth.

When the particular moths in the test emerged, 77 percent of them avoided ethyl acetate, and that group was made of individual moths that had pupated from the same caterpillars who had learned avoidance.

These caterpillars were melted down to proteins, and *still*, the knowledge of what to fear was passed on to the moth. I may not have gone through a primordial soup phase, but maybe my snake phobia is stamped on some molecular building block from before me. It's a thought, anyway. Whatever the case, I somehow made it past the snake spot and pressed on.

I still held that the waterfall was more a tiered pool. But it was beautiful, especially on a sunny day. A small clearing among giant trees with cool water bubbling over the rocks. I looked up, and the reflections from the water were dancing across the underside of heliconia leaves. Profilio had his butterfly net. Moody had his camera. They were both happily stalking. Jordan was swiveling her head around, taking in the jungle. She usually speaks in complete sentences, but she only kept saying, "Oh my God. You guys. Oh my God. Beautiful."

It was the opposite Belizean jungle experience of her special-ops friend who had gone catatonic in a tree.

Thirteen

THE MITCHELL-HEDGES CRYSTAL SKULL

I was scrambling over ancient stones trying to find the supposed excavation site of the crystal skull so I could tell Jordan the story in the right setting. We had planned another visit to the Chaos Oasis during her visit, and I wanted her to be prepared.

It was easy to get turned around at Lubaantun. The grounds were an immaculate green park stretching over forty acres, shaded by giant ceiba trees with spreading canopies. But the ruins themselves were mostly a tumbled-down jumble. There were only a few explanatory signs about what we were looking at.

Researchers believe the site was inhabited for about 160 years sometime after 730 CE and then abandoned at the same time Mayan cities across the southern lowlands suddenly collapsed.

The buildings were erected using black slate, which was different than the limestone more typically used in Mayan construction. The blocks were set together without any type of mortar, and the buildings had rounded corners, which was highly unusual.

When the ground shifted in an earthquake or some other major event, the buildings had crumbled. It didn't help that in 1917 British Honduras sent Dr. Thomas Gann, their chief medical officer and an amateur archeologist, to excavate the site. He used dynamite to haphazardly blow things up in his hunt for priceless treasures.

Earlier in our stay, Moody and I had hired Geronimo, a newly licensed guide from the village who often stood at the crossroads hoping to flag down the occasional tourist.

By then, we had explored Lubaantun's nooks and crannies. We knew our way around the ball courts and down to the river. I had spent a couple of afternoons seated in front of a small fan in the hot, closet-size office of Appolinario, the park's head ranger, as he discussed Lubaantun's history. His employer, the government, didn't allow him to give tours, which was a pity since he knew the place the way his uncle Sebastian knew the butterfly farm.

We hired young Geronimo mostly because we saw him standing in the heat every day next to a little-traveled road. I told Geronimo that he didn't need to give us the whole rundown. I was more interested in his personal connections to the site as someone who had grown up next door.

But Geronimo gripped the lanyard holding his official photo ID and gave us a tour befitting the crowd he seemed to be envisioning.

"Listen up, everybody," he shouted to Moody and me at each ball court and plaza before rattling off dates.

When we got to the place where he said the crystal skull was discovered, he went off script. Guide school materials taught that the whole story was a hoax. But Geronimo said he knew better because his great-grandfather had been there that day.

For any of this to make sense, the story is essential, so *listen up, everybody*.

The Mitchell-Hedges Crystal Skull

In 1924 (or 1926, by some accounts) Thomas Gann of the explosive archeological-digging techniques returned to Lubaantun with British

Museum expedition leader F. A. Mitchell-Hedges, the future radio host who told tales of being attacked by vicious iguanas, discovering lost civilizations in the Amazon, fighting with Pancho Villa in Mexico, and unwittingly rooming with Leon Trotsky in New York City shortly before the Russian revolution.

The story told by Mitchell-Hedges's daughter, Anna, was that she was along on this expedition.

On her seventeenth birthday, she climbed a pyramid at Lubaantun and from there could see an unearthly glow in the excavation site. She climbed down, using a rope and dropping past scorpions. She swept dirt off an altar and, there, discovered the crystal skull.

It was a block of clear quartz about five inches tall, and later, they found its detachable jaw. Her father said it was called the Skull of Doom.

"It is at least 3,600 years old and, according to legend, used by the High Priest of the Maya when performing esoteric rites," Mitchell-Hedges wrote. "It is said that when he willed death with the skull, death invariably followed. It has been described as the embodiment of evil."

In the eighties, a Canadian psychic said the skull had a more positive purpose. In a series of taped sessions, approved of by Anna Mitchell-Hedges, Carole Davis communed with the skull. Through her, it said it was made by beings of higher intelligence thousands of years before the Maya. (All the space-alien-ancient-treasure theories are considered racist because they indicate white people find it easier to believe aliens pulled off an engineering or artistic feat than to give credit to indigenous people. You don't hear folks claiming the Roman aqueducts were built by intergalactic beings.)

The skull told Davis that it was a portal to shared universal wisdom.

"This receptacle contains the minds of many and minds of one," the medium said in a staccato voice, channeling the skull.

An online site called Strange Mag gives the recordings of her sessions a thumbs-up: "Her speaking for the skull is fascinating to listen to, for she commences each trance with unearthly shrieks."

Anna once said she had harnessed the skull's powers to kill a man. But after it turned out to be a portal to cosmic wisdom, she credited the skull's healing powers for her long life—she lived to one hundred years old. The current owner has renamed it the Skull of Love.

And, yes, there is an Indiana Jones movie where Indy chases the Mitchell-Hedges crystal skull to a secret temple and inter-dimensional beings trying to return home.

It is a totally awesome story. The only problem is that the skull has been proven to be phony six ways to Sunday. Marks indicate it was made with rotary tools not invented until the twentieth century. It's believed to have been manufactured in Germany. There's proof Mitchell-Hedges bought it in 1943 from an art dealer for four hundred pounds. There is no evidence that Anna was ever in Belize.

Yet, the crystal skull legend flourishes. On eBay, you can buy a book that describes the true powers of the skull and how scientists have tried to hide its authenticity. Order now and you get two free DVDs.

You can even have a personal piece of the power. In a "private setting on Earth Day 2020," the Mitchell-Hedges skull energized a small group of crystals, according to a sales site. These crystals can be "worn as a pendant, or suspended over an altar, over your bed, in your car, your healing table, etc. so you can benefit from the extraordinary power and energy of the amazing Mitchell-Hedges Crystal Skull."

They are only thirty-five dollars, and each is faceted at the back so it "sparkles with light!" You also get a cord and pouch to carry it in.

I was tempted to do my Christmas shopping in one fell swoop when I saw the purchase included the pouch.

Moody, Jordan, and I were eating our lunch in the shade where I thought Geronimo had said the excavation took place. Although it wasn't like I had to swear allegiance to accuracy, as I was looking for the site of an event that hadn't happened—or, at best, was staged.

This was just the first part of the story I wanted to tell Jordan before we visited the Chaos Oasis.

The second part was the day Moody saved me from awkwardness. It was on one of our early visits with Alisa at Chaos Oasis. From the get-go, I had found her fun. So I thought we were joking around as we talked about Thomas Gann and Mitchell-Hedges and the crystal skull.

"Gann gets such criticism, but you have to consider the times," Alisa said.

"Right," I agreed. "What's a few explosions when looking for pottery?"

Alisa said the crystal quartz of the Mitchell-Hedges skull had a certain vibration that activated a little-used part of the brain.

"Yes," I said, "I hear it also bestows tap-dancing skills," but Alisa's head was in the refrigerator, and I then saw Moody across the room shaking his head and waving his hand across his throat like a director saying "Cut!" Alisa was still distracted, so I used my eyebrows to silently ask Moody, "Why?"

His eyes directed my gaze to the many crystal skulls everywhere, from napkin rings to refrigerator magnets.

I silently made an expression that I hoped said, "C'mon, it's just kitsch, they aren't serious."

He shrugged and raised his eyebrows in that "I don't know, but I'd be careful" way.

I was careful after that detailed conversation. I didn't want to offend someone who had been kind enough to send us off with homemade preserves and a bottle of colloidal silver. Also, I didn't want to be closed-minded, even about things like extraterrestrial quartz carvers.

Just as I finished warning Jordan that we should tread carefully yet learn all we could if we visited Chaos Oasis, I got a text from Alisa saying she was home and we were welcome to visit.

That afternoon, we sat in the coolness of the Crystal Skull bar drinking fresh lemonade. Jordan steered the conversation to Mitchell-Hedges.

Alisa said it was true Mitchell-Hedges had bought the skull at an auction in the forties. But he'd actually excavated it before then. He gave it to a friend as collateral on a loan and came up with the money just in time to buy it back after his friend listed it for auction.

I asked why the crystal skull was kept in Indiana.

Alisa said that's where their friend had his karate studio but he did travel with it.

I said Appolinario thought the skull, real or fake, belonged at Lubaantun.

Alisa disagreed. She said that, the day before she died, Anna Mitchell-Hedges had entrusted the skull to their friend Bill Homann, who had cared for Anna in the last eight years of her life.

He married Anna Mitchell-Hedges when she was ninety-two. There were forty years between them. But Alisa said they were really more close friends and the marriage was for health insurance.

That night, Jordan and I were in the kitchen where the Wi-Fi signal was stronger. We had some Internet sleuthing to do.

First up, we found a photo of Bill Homann. There he was in a promotional shot for a showing of the crystal skull. He was mustachioed, wearing a safari jacket, scarf, and an Indiana Jones fedora.

I studied his face and considered whether my next stop should be a karate studio in Indiana. If he was a true believer, it might not be interesting, but what if he was the latest in an unbroken line of inventive hoaxers and wanted to talk about it? Did that connect to Fallen Stones?

Jordan looked at him and said, "You know, he reminds me of the guy at that weird sex cult in Hawaii where I accidentally stayed."

"Excuse me?" I asked. It turned out that, during the same winter break that Moody and I had gone to Belize to have a big fight on the beach and discover Fallen Stones, Jordan, who isn't opposed to things like healing energies, went to Hawaii.

I might complain from time to time about my little hurt feelings and trouble fitting in during the fellowship, but the experience had been much harder on Jordan. She was shouldering heavy personal grief and hoping for some breathing room during the time we shared in that hothouse of future leaders.

Lane, a soldier she loved, had been killed in combat, and even though his death had occurred years ago, Jordan had just been pretending to hold it together. She was carrying that loss and needed to take time to heal. Before the winter break, she went online and saw a gorgeous off-grid retreat in Hawaii offering peace, love, and understanding. She sent a deposit. Something about the photo of a wild, empty cliff and the stretching sea called to her. She was too tired and desperate to do serious research that might have unearthed the fact that it had been a sex cult in the seventies before becoming a chichi renewal spa in the new century under the same ownership. She just read the reviews of women who had allegedly found some peace there and booked.

When she arrived, after a steep and twisty three-hour drive, a strangely silent person in a monk's robe led her to the guy she took to be the manager. He placed his hand on her upper chest and put her hand on his chest so they could "read each other's hearts."

"Why would you do that?" I asked.

"It was so weird that I just wanted to see where it was going," she said. "I wasn't in any danger. He was old-old."

When they were finished reading, she went to her glamping tent for a nap, and while she was sleeping, the old-old man entered, carrying towels.

Jordan leapt to her feet in a martial-arts position, poised for attack.

The man set down the towels; put his arms straight out, palms up; closed his eyes; and nodded.

"I sense within you a warrior spirit," he told Jordan, who thought, *Very insightful, Sherlock, as you came very close to having your head kicked off.*

She secured her cottage and made sure she would know if anyone came near again by leaving little telltales around in specific places. Each time she returned to her room or woke, she checked to be sure they hadn't moved. It was a trick she supposedly knew from watching spy movies. She had gathered the place was weird, but she didn't really care because the grounds were wild and beautiful and she could take care of herself. There were plenty of ordinary-looking guests walking about in cushioned sneakers and sun hats.

The next day on a walk, she came to a beautiful open-beamed studio on a cliff with a panoramic view of the Pacific Ocean. Inside, there were yoga mats in a basket, modern-art mobiles drifting in the breeze, and a sign that said: "Welcome. Breathe." No one else was around.

She went in and lay on a mat and just breathed. She saw Lane's face. She heard his voice. And, finally, after years of pretending to be okay, she cried. She cried and cried and cried, and then, her face still wet with tears, her breath still jagged, she felt the slightest flicker of reassurance, she felt life seeping back into her. She opened her eyes and focused on the mobiles—and slowly recognized the figures of gigantic phalluses twirling around, dangling from the ceiling.

And just like that, she laughed. She laughed and knew it was the exact kind of thing that Lane would have found hysterical.

Moody was reading in the room above the kitchen where he heard us laughing and me saying, *"Penis mobiles?"*

He came down to see what he was missing. The three of us decided to have cocktails in the kitchen, out of reach, we hoped, of some of the mosquitoes, even though we propped the door open because of the heat.

Moody was sitting in a chair at the end of the room, farthest from the door.

Jordan was sitting on the counter, and I was leaning against the refrigerator. We were holding drinks and chatting about the day when the bat flew in. It happened so fast. It seemed to go straight for Moody. Then swooped out.

"Are you bit?" I screamed. "Is there blood?"

Jordan used her serious voice.

"If that bat even touched you, you need a rabies shot."

Moody claimed it had not touched him.

Jordan and I ditched our search for Mr. Crystal Skull and started researching bat dangers instead:

Google Search

Do bats bite?

Can you tell if a bat bit you?

What to do if a bat touches you?

"I thought they were supposed to have radar!" I said.

"They do. That's why it didn't touch me and you two need to settle down," Moody said. "But, Jordan, do you have a plan if a rabid bat comes back?"

"I'm going home tomorrow," Jordan said. "You're on your own."

I kept scrolling our current repository of shared universal knowledge, my phone, not certain whether I considered the World Wide Web a skull of doom or love.

Looking up bats led me to articles on vampires, which led me to reading about Dracula, which made me think of the crystal skull again.

Legends and myths, they have such staying power. It's like people just want to believe in something of another realm. The idea that there were so many people—karate teachers in Indiana and Belizeans alike—hanging on to a mystical skull of storied powers didn't seem too odd, even if I couldn't quite get on board. There were things we all needed to believe to move forward. I wanted to believe that somewhere out there, the spirit of Jordan and Lane had shared a good laugh over a big dick mobile wafting in an island breeze.

Fourteen

Birthday Parties

The usually dignified Sebastian had a secret. Sometimes on the weekends, he drank too many Belikins, and when he did, he became a sentimental sap. He would call Clive in England and tell him he loved him. He would text Moody and tell him that we were good people and that we made the house happy. He was another one who felt the house had been lonely.

During one of these wee-hour exchanges, he invited us to the birthday party for his wife, Hovita.

I was excited. Only men worked at the butterfly farm. I'd questioned Sebastian about that fact, and he said he had hired women in the past but they didn't stay long because they didn't like touching caterpillars.

I vigorously attacked such sexist nonsense but was somewhat undermined by the fact that, at the time we were having the conversation, I was using a pair of tweezers to pick up squishy caterpillars. Still, I was hardly a representative sampling.

Now, finally, I would have a chance to meet some of the women in the village. I had only briefly met Hovita when we'd dropped Sebastian off at home weeks before.

"We better wait and see if Sebastian remembers," Moody said, squinting at his phone. "He just texted that he loved me."

The days went by, but we heard nothing further from a sober Sebastian about a party. The day of Hovita's birthday, I gave up hope. It looked like I was going to have to do laundry in the river if I wanted to hang out with the women of San Pedro Columbia.

Then we got a text from Sebastian telling us he would come to the house at noon so we could drive to the village for Hovita's birthday lunch.

When we got there, we were ushered into the concrete house. Sebastian waved for us to sit at a table with three chairs. The white tablecloth was embroidered with gold-thread butterflies.

Sebastian sat down with us.

Marthe, their daughter, came over from the thatch house with Spanish chicken escabeche and filled our bowls. It was a specialty of Hovita's, and it was delicious: sweet and vinegary, made with carrots and onions from their garden. For this, I decided immediately as the smell hit my nostrils, I would eat chicken. If only we'd had an escabeche invitation when Kat and Jed were visiting. I was going to ask everything about making it because my friend Jeanne in Fresno would want to know. She's a master Southern cook, and she likes to learn everything she can about other cultures' home cooking. I'd already sent her a local cook's recipe for Belizean black beans and rice with coconut milk.

Eager to get the recipe and some quality time, I asked when Hovita would be joining us. Sebastian said she would come later. She was visiting with her older daughters. Hovita had wanted Sebastian to bring us for lunch one day, and he'd decided her birthday, when she already had family over, was a good day to do it. I had a feeling he hadn't consulted Hovita on this. Moody asked Sebastian if people in the village ever had parties with groups of people for their birthdays.

Sebastian said, oh, yes, his brothers-in-law had thrown him a big barbecue on his birthday.

At the end of the meal the three of us shared, Hovita arrived and hovered in the doorway. We showered the meal with compliments, dropped off a small gift, and then Sebastian told us he needed to get back to work. Hovita seemed out of reach to me, but I knew that it was only because I hadn't spent enough time with her. Sebastian had been very formal at first, and now we were one of his drunk dials. Marthe, Hovita's look-alike, who came each week to clean and make tortillas, had been very quiet and dignified at the beginning. She had the best posture of anyone I'd ever met. But now I knew about her days waiting tables at the Tipsy Tuna Sports Bar in Placencia and how she ranked the world's citizens based on her experiences serving them beers. (She liked South Africans best. Americans landed overall in the middle because they were either the best or the worst, which was a take I agreed with, and she had trouble understanding what Brits were saying. Again, I agreed.) It had been my and Moody's dismal attempts at tortilla shaping that had made her laugh and relax, except for her perfect posture.

But we left that day without getting to know Hovita much better. She'd made us a delicious meal, and we'd spent time in her home, but it was clear she had other birthday visitors to attend to. I was determined to spend time with her later.

I didn't fare any better than Hovita on my birthday. Moody wasn't one for making a fuss. But I had decided that, instead of silently nursing a martyr complex, I would proactively manage the situation. Before we ever left California, I told him that we would be in Belize on my birthday—so many possible ways to celebrate! I may have shown him a photo of a Francis Ford Coppola resort.

Since then, thoughts of swanky escapes had disappeared from my mind. James and Sarka had been right. Anyone could stay at a resort. How often did you get to live at a butterfly farm in the jungle? I wanted to soak in all I could. But I still made sure to mention my birthday several times in the weeks leading up to it, thoughtfully protecting Moody from forgetting and me from being hurt.

He didn't forget. When I opened my eyes that morning, still groggy, he was sitting up, alert.

"Happy birthday!" he said.

He then looked relieved like a man who had remembered that, yes, he had locked the garage before leaving the house and could check it off his list of worries. He gave me a perfunctory kiss, picked up his iPad, and started reading.

My heart sank. I started doing that breathing thing I do when I don't want to feel my emotions: *Breathe in, breathe out. Look at that interesting shadow on the wall. What's that old song? "It's my birthday and I'll cry if I want to"*—no, breathe in, breathe out.

After a while, Moody went to make coffee. I heard clattering and could tell he was making breakfast as well. I felt relief. I felt happiness. I was already writing the story in my head that we'd be telling in the future:

"Remember that birthday in the jungle far from any stores? And you walked in with a tray and there was a vase of heliconia and a breakfast of . . ."

(Here, my imagination had to pause and think because I knew we were low on groceries. We were down to dried goods. Hmm—we had oatmeal!)

"You walked in with a bowl of oatmeal because it was all we had left, but you'd made a heart out of raisins, and I felt so loved and . . ."

My fantasy was interrupted by gray reality. Moody came in, slamming the door quickly because the mosquitoes were swarming.

"I made oatmeal. Want some?" he said. "We should eat in here. It's really buggy today."

There was oatmeal in a pot. Its glutinous globs spilled over the edge. There were raisins in a box. There were no jungle flowers.

So, I thought, this was to be my life. No romantic highs. No raisin hearts. Just a bowl of nourishing gruel served from a pot. This is what happens when you get old.

I sat up to eat, crossing my legs and balancing a bowl on my lap, and thought about the night before my fourteenth birthday. A boy that liked me brought his guitar to my house and sang, "Hey, Deanie, won't you come out tonight?" beneath my bedroom window.

Only, he changed Deanie to "Dee-eed," a drawn-out version of my nickname. He also got the wrong window, waking my parents.

My dad had to come to my room.

"First of all, you're too young to date, young lady. That is *not* going to happen. Second, that boy can't sing. And that song is terrible. You are going to clean up this pigsty of a room in the morning and listen to Johnny Cash the whole time!"

It was terribly romantic. That memory made me think of other birthdays when I was really little. The ballerina cake. The Lite Brite—you could make pictures with lit-up pegs! I was born on Groundhog Day before it became a movie. On my birthday, my parents would wake me and carry me in my footed pajamas to the couch in front of the television to see if Punxsutawney Phil predicted an early spring. This was an event that news stations actually used to broadcast live: men in top hats pulling out a rodent and asking for weather predictions. But I was a little confused in my early years and thought the men were dressed up because it was *my* birthday.

And, now, here I was, a middle-aged woman eating undecorated oatmeal out of reach of the mosquitoes. *It all goes so fast. Spring is gone, Phil.*

Reality beckoned. We had to go to PG to get supplies.

I was quiet on the drive. *(Breathe. Breathe.)*

"Why are you being so quiet?" Moody asked. "There aren't real stores here. You didn't expect me to buy you something?"

I decided to risk honesty while trying not to show my hurt feelings.

"It's not about *buying* things," I said with an oh-so-casual shrug. "It's just that if it were the other way around, I would have maybe put your oatmeal in a bowl and made a heart with raisins."

"You wanted me to make a heart with raisins?" Moody asked incredulously. "Raisins!" he said, shaking his head in bewildered disapproval.

Luckily, we had arrived at the San Pedro Columbia home of David, who helmed the butterfly farm closer to Hickatee. We didn't get to see him as often as the others. He'd invited us to visit his family on our way to town.

I slipped quickly out of the Jeep to escape being mocked for wanting a romantic gesture in the form of dried fruit.

I was immediately swarmed by children. David's youngest, a tiny sprig of a girl barely past toddlerhood, in a dress printed with big purple roses, wrapped herself around my leg and stayed there even when I was walking.

David and Clementa had four children, but their cousins lived next door, so there was always a playground full of kids running between houses.

On an earlier trip, I'd given the kids a set of jacks. (Packing tip: stuff your suitcase with children's books and inexpensive toys to give away when traveling.) Many little hands pulled me inside to sit in a circle and play a game.

Even when you are old and unloved, playing jacks with laughing children can cheer your listless heart.

David and Clementa's house was one big room with hammocks in the center, although they were beginning to build walls inside and had just ordered bay windows from a Mennonite community. (Mennonites had settled in Belize in the 1950s and were known for their carpentry and dairy skills.)

The kids decided to braid my hair. David Jr. borrowed my phone to take photos of their handiwork.

It's always nice to get your hair done and take some snapshots on your birthday.

Sitting on the hammock like he was riding a horse, David told us about an incredible experience he'd had that week. He'd seen a jaguar.

Very few people lay eyes on a wild jaguar. Sebastian had told Moody and me that we shouldn't even dream of a sighting—there were, no doubt, jaguars passing through Fallen Stones, but we would never spot one. They were the ghosts of the forest.

The big cats—the largest and most powerful in the western hemisphere—have a gold coat with black rosettes, each one as distinct as a human fingerprint, and glowing eyes as gold as their coat. Sometimes they are born with a black coat—a panther—but even then, the rosette pattern still shows.

Cockscomb Basin, the world's first jaguar preserve, was located in Belize, and conservationists were passionately working to make it part of an international corridor from Mexico to Argentina. The jaguar, a species that had once roamed as far north as Arizona and California, had already lost more than half of its range.

I'd seen footage from a field camera hidden at Cockscomb. The jaguar had walked past the camera, and instead of merely blending into the woods like a regular animal, its markings had made the outer edges blur into the background so it was erased while it walked past—an apparition that vanished before your eyes.

But David had seen a jaguar in broad daylight. The new branch of the farm where he worked was a prototype. Clive had sketched out some fanciful ideas. Sebastian had added a practicality wish list, then Eduardo had brought his engineering skills. Instead of dim, cramped huts, the two buildings had towering termite-free steel frames, a strong zinc roof, and windows all around to let in light so the host plants could grow where the butterflies lived. The windows had strong metal mesh screens to keep out ants and other threats. It incorporated the latest in butterfly farm design.

David worked alone and missed being around Sebastian and the others, but he did have unobstructed views of jungle life. He also had the advantage of being safely behind glass and steel mesh when the jaguar strolled by, though he may not have needed the protection. Jaguars are powerful predators that can crush a skull with one bite. But there is little evidence that, unprovoked, wild jaguars attack humans.

Alan Rabinowitz, an American zoologist who cofounded Panthera, the organization behind the push for an international jaguar corridor, was once tracking a jaguar in Belize for research. The cat circled around and started tracking him until they came face to face.

Rabinowitz had to decide what to do.

"I could get big and scream and act crazy, but the cat wasn't doing anything—it was just walking and curious," he said in a 2018 *Atlantic* article. "So I kneeled. And the jaguar sat, which was not what I expected."

After a while, Rabinowitz stood up and backed away. The jaguar got up and also walked away, looking back over its shoulder in a non-deadly adieu.

The jaguar was sacred to the ancient Maya, a symbol of power. This designation hadn't always been a good thing for the jaguars.

Near the fall of the great Mesoamerica Mayan Empire, the land was deforested, and a great drought was intensified as the ruling class used natural resources for their palaces. There was widespread disease, evidenced by archeologists' discovery of a great many graves of children and adolescents.

In this time of trauma, Yax Pasaj Chan Yopaat, the last king of the Mayan city of Copán in what is now Honduras, built an altar at the foot of a thirty-foot pyramid. It showed him as a divine ruler receiving the scepter from the founding ruler, even though he was not related to that dynasty.

In front of the carved slab of stone known as Altar Q, priests sacrificed sixteen jaguars and pumas, one for each king, creating a spectacle to legitimize Yax Pasaj.

In 2018, archeologist Nawa Sugiyama did groundbreaking research using chemical analysis of the excavated bones to discover the cats had been fed birds that ate corn, which meant the cats were held in captivity.

The breathtaking animals were once revered as gods by Maya who lived in close contact with nature. But these jaguars may have been captured as far away as Belize, then held before being ritually sacrificed as an act of propaganda to prop up a king who cared only for his standing with the ruling class and saw all others as expendable.

Soon after, the empire's cities were abandoned, and a vast, complex, advanced civilization disappeared. Because, and I say this in a higher register with ever-quickening words: how-long-can-a-society-that-destroys-the-natural-world-and-systematically-oppresses-the-masses-and-sacrifices-human-lives-and-subverts-the-very-essence-of-all-that-was-once-held-sacred-survive? Excuse me, I may have misdirected my burning rage by a millennia or so.

It was the Mayan Empire that crumbled—the system, the architecture, the government. The Mayan people lived on and endured through centuries. There are approximately five million Maya alive in the world today.

The jaguar has survived too.

One of the threats to the species is a throwback to Yax Pasaj trying to cloak himself in their majesty. There is a black market for jaguar teeth and other body parts peddled as an amulet mystically imparting power and virility.

Yet, even with freeways and cities and a dark-hearted trade for animal body parts, there are still remaining swaths of jungle, and jaguar ghosts still roam—and David had seen one in daylight.

David flashed his infectious smile while describing its beauty. His face looked almost as full of wonder as those of his children, who were listening to the story.

Fifteen

A Love Story and a Leader

I promised Sammy that if I wrote about him, I would use Manuel "Sammy" Cal, which is how he wants his name to appear in butterfly books someday when he is known for discovering many species. I use different names for different worlds, so I—Diana "Deed" Marcum—could relate.

Moody and I only knew him as Manuel for the first month. He was thirty but as kinetic as a kid on a playground. He could easily climb a palm tree for coconuts. He was always laughing, unless Moody tried to photograph him. Then he went somber and tight-lipped because he was self-conscious about a missing front tooth. I was curious about his stand on recreational drug use, as one day, he would wear a "D.A.R.E. to Resist Drugs" T-shirt and, the next day, a T-shirt with a marijuana leaf on it. He bought his work clothes at the secondhand shop in PG.

He invited us to his house near the river. On our way there, we got turned around and kept asking people in San Pedro Columbia where Manuel lived. Everyone shrugged and put up their palms until someone said, "He lives by the river? He works at the butterfly farm? Oh! You mean Sammy."

Sammy, we found out, was a name he'd liked when he was little, and he'd given it to himself.

Moody could also relate. When he was a kid, he'd dreamed of being called Mike. Baseball players, apparently, were predominantly named Mike when Moody was a child. Another friend of mine recalls wishing to be named Celery, although she can't remember why. Sammy had made his childhood dreams of a name change a reality.

When we finally found Sammy's house, he was outside unloading lumber. He'd lost his tooth in an accident on a friend's motorcycle and had to decide whether to go to Guatemala and get it fixed or buy the lumber. He couldn't afford both, even though he made good money by village standards.

He decided to continue with his house building. He said he was young and could get his tooth fixed later. I thought of Gareth, the man I'd met at the Florida butterfly conference who had decided he was too old to get his front tooth fixed. Dentists must struggle.

Sammy's mother, Petrona, was making tortillas on a comal, a cast-iron griddle. She had it heating on a low rock stove over an open flame beneath their thatch roof. Hanging on the wall was a colander made from a polished gourd that looked like a work of art. Sammy was puzzled by my admiration. It was as if someone came to my house and oohed-and-aahed over my salad spinner. Catarino, a local craftsman, who worked as a groundskeeper at Lubaantun, had made the colander and also their bowls and spoons.

Catarino had a side trade in ceramics. At Lubaantun when the workers were mowing, they pretty regularly discovered pieces of artifacts, usually broken carved whistles. Appolinario kept them unceremoniously on shelves in the office.

Tourists begged to buy them, sometimes offering more than park workers made in a month. Removing antiquities from Belize was illegal, and also personally repulsive to Appolinario and Catarino. They bristled at the Mayan treasures that had never been returned by American and British museums.

Catarino studied photos of Mayan art and the pieces of antiquities they kept on the shelves and started sculpting copies. He was using the same earth and the same techniques as the ancient Maya. He sold them to tourists, carving his initials and the date on the bottom so no one got arrested for forgery or smuggling.

Sammy's four-year-old daughter, Aricelly Elsa—"We gave her two names too!" Sammy said—wanted to fake swordplay with Moody and me on the stairwell of an old church next door.

"Come hear the ghosts sing," she said.

"Don't worry," Sammy told us. "They only sing at night, and that was a long time ago."

Sammy's history was intertwined with Fallen Stones. His father had worked five years on the crew building the road for the farm. His mother is Sebastian's sister. His older sister Amelia worked at the bar during the years they'd tried to make Fallen Stones a rustic resort.

Amelia had worried about bad men seeing her walk alone on that steep road. So, from the time he was ten years old until he was fourteen, Sammy walked his sister and the other girls to the farm.

He was already in love with butterflies by the time he made it up the hill. His mother grew flowers around their house to attract them, and as a child, he chased them with an old clothes basket.

Sammy did well in school but had to leave at thirteen because his family couldn't afford to send him to the next level. He desperately wanted a job at the butterfly farm. Then he could learn the scientific names of the butterflies he'd already learned to recognize by sight. He could make a name for himself.

After the hurricane and the fire, there were no job openings at the farm for many years. But the butterfly farm slowly crawled back, and in 2014, when Sammy was twenty-four, Sebastian finally offered him a job.

A couple of years later, Sammy's father died. They hadn't been close, and Sammy said that made it harder. On the day of his father's burial ceremony, a friend tried to ease his spirits and said, "Let's go for a drive." They drove to San Antonio, the beautiful Mopan village in the hills to the west, and that's the day he first saw Ilvina.

"I went, *whoa*!" Sammy told me. It was, I noted, his word of choice for elusive butterflies and love at first sight.

He went up to her and asked if he could spend time with her. She said no, she didn't want to give him her phone number.

He was leaving when she changed her mind.

They texted and secretly dated for a year. He told her he was going by himself to her parents to ask for her partnership.

The tradition was for his parents to go to her parents and ask for the daughter to come live with their family. But Sammy didn't have his father, his mother only spoke Kekchi, and her family were traditional Mopan Maya.

He went to Ilvina's house himself and made his case. Her mother told him no. She said they didn't want him for their daughter.

Ilvina said she was going anyway. She was leaving with him right then.

In that moment, Sammy saw how much she loved him. But since her family was traditional, leaving without their consent could ban her from them.

He told a sobbing Ilvina, "You are my match. We are a pair. I love you with my heart and in my gut. I will come back. I will make them want me in your family."

He came back with his mother.

Her family still said no. They said they had heard that he came from a poor and rough family. They felt their family was more upstanding.

Sammy told them that poor and rough are not the same thing and his family was the best family and that he had a good job and was going to be very successful. This time, Ilvina left with him.

While he told the story, Ilvina and Petrona nodded emphatically. Aricelly was wide-eyed. She hadn't heard the story before. But I bet she would soon know every word.

Ilvina's family had apologized and had come around to treating Sammy well. It had been on a trip to San Antonio, taking Aricelly to visit her grandparents, that he saw that little striped butterfly lay her eggs. It was the turning point in what I thought of as Sammy's Quest.

He had seventy-five of the *Aeria eurimedia* now. Their pupating time was too short to send in the regular box. But if Clive returned to Belize, he could take the pupae back with him on a more direct flight.

Sebastian was hoping to use the *Aeria eurimedia* as a lure to get Clive to come and stay for a month. Sebastian wanted to show Clive all the details of the operation and have him get to know each worker, because Sebastian had started thinking about succession.

He'd been at the butterfly farm for thirty years. He was only fifty-one, but it was a sore, limping fifty-one. The year before, he had taken a bad fall riding his bicycle down the hill. It had left him cautious on his daily ride. He wanted Clive to buy a truck for the farm.

"But you don't drive," I pointed out.

"I think it's not so hard," said Sebastian.

The fall had also made him think about what would happen to the farm if he wasn't there.

One day at the blue morpho flight house, I asked Sebastian how he defined good leadership.

He went so still, thinking, that the butterflies began alighting on him.

One thing that I already knew about Sebastian was that he believed in choosing his words carefully when the subject was important to him.

"Do you think everyone here gets along and they all love me?" Sebastian asked.

"Yes, that's exactly what I think," I said, in my mind replaying how the chattering and giggling woke me up every morning as the guys came down to work and how respectfully the younger ones would tell me that "Mr. Sebastian said this" or "Mr. Sebastian taught me that."

Sebastian said there was grumbling over decisions, some who thought they knew better than him, and some who had complaints about one another. He said when these things arose, it was his job to show no sign of having heard the gossip or rumor until someone came to him directly. Then he had to address the problem by speaking nicely to each involved party and never raise his voice.

"To put yourself into leadership means you have a very big responsibility," said Sebastian, looking serious even by Sebastian standards of straight face.

"You have to show by example that you know how to do the work, you know how to keep the project going, you know how to make the project grow. You have to show all the time that you are committed, and then you are a good leader and your people will follow."

He said he wanted to create more jobs for people in the village and that he wanted Fallen Stones to be there for their children and their children's children.

"Do you think the world will last that long?" I asked, giving away my anxieties.

"Much longer," said Sebastian. "The decision we must make is: What kind of world?"

Walking back to the house, I thought about how the closest thing I'd witnessed to a personality clash on the farm had made me laugh.

Moody and I had once remarked on Profilio's poetic nature within earshot of Malvin.

Malvin, as everyone acknowledged, was the one with the handsome face. He was a champion soccer player and had the strong-silent-type thing down pat. He made even Moody and Sebastian seem like chatterboxes.

"Profilio is a quote machine," Moody said.

"I want to remember everything he's ever told us," I replied.

"I used to work with Profilio when I was a groundskeeper," Malvin interjected. "He is a radio that can't be turned off."

One evening, instead of our usual sunset viewing, Moody and I drove to Lubaantun. Appolinario and Catarino didn't mind if we took a walk after the posted hours as long as we were out the gates by the time they left. One of the tensions with the villagers and our British neighbor Richard was that he would walk Lubaantun by a full moon, which he said he found spiritual, and which they found arrogant. From his point of view, he was hardly a tourist. He lived next door. From their point of view, he had already built a Chaos Oasis next door to Mayan ruins. He could respect their closing hours. Also, Appolinario didn't have much respect for people whose interest in Lubaantun was centered around the crystal skull—with the exception of one tourist who had visited earlier in the year.

The man had run up to the office, screaming, "I found it! I found it!"

Appolinario came out and first saw the man's children in fits of giggles, then saw the man on his knees holding aloft one of the cartoonish crystal skull mugs they sold at the airport. Appolinario thought that man was clever.

I had an ulterior motive for the Lubaantun trip that evening. I wanted to buy one of Catarino's whistles, the clay sculptures of warriors in jaguar headdresses, and other figures that were copies of real artifacts found at Lubaantun, but it turned out to be his day off. Moody suggested we go to San Pedro Columbia. Sammy had mentioned Catarino lived near him and that he sold his little sculptures from his house.

We stopped at Sammy's to ask directions. Sammy's teenage nephew said he'd come with us and show us the way. Aricelly jumped up and down and said she wanted to come too and climbed in. Sammy decided he would also join, then Ilvina squeezed in. All six of us drove three houses down.

Catarino's daughters were out front sorting beans. His wife was making tortillas on a comal. Catarino, looking off duty in shorts and a pair of Crocs, waved us all into their courtyard. We used upside-down plastic buckets for chairs. A daughter-in-law brought out juices, and we all watched while Catarino showed us how he made his whistles. He mixed the mud, shaped and patted it, then sketched in the designs with a tool that was modeled after the tools the ancient Maya had used.

The warrior he was sculpting would have to be dried and fired. He brought out the ones he had already made. Moody, of course, chose a ballplayer. I didn't see one right for me. Catarino said something in Kekchi to one of his daughters. She went inside and brought out a little clay sculpture with the face of a Mayan person in profile. He (or I prefer to think "she") was wearing a rabbit headdress. Catarino told me the rabbit often symbolized a writer or scribe. If I turned it around, the other side was a whistle.

Catarino had made this small ceramic so his kids could take it to school on show-and-tell day. All the older siblings had used it, and this year, the youngest was taking it to class the next day. But I could buy it and Sammy could bring it to the house after its final classroom appearance. I agreed, happy to have found the whistle right for me.

Sixteen

MANY TOUCANS

The changes at Fallen Stones came continually—orange Julia butterflies replaced by dozens of glasswing butterflies flitting about like airborne crystals, water vines growing as if before my eyes.

It was February, and Sebastian said the best was yet to come. By April, the cicadas would be singing, and when you looked at the valley from the top, it would be a bowl of yellow from the flowering quamwood trees.

"Won't it be hot?" I asked him.

Sebastian shrugged.

Profilio was working near the house, building a new flight house for some of the butterfly species they were trying to breed. Malvin had caught a butterfly that was purple and gold, a *Caligo uranus*, a gold-edged owl butterfly. It looked like it was half sunflower. Malvin told me that when he saw the butterfly, he said, "I got you now."

Profilio was becoming a feminist, although he probably wouldn't use that word. I couldn't wait to hear his latest revelation.

It had begun when he watched a tiny, older mestizo woman who favored bright-turquoise dresses take her produce to market in a long-nosed dugout that she guided down the Columbia River with poles pushed into the river bottom. Sometimes in the rainy season, even young men would chicken out before taking a dory on the river. But this woman, Zenovia, came down each day, and Profilio had watched from afar.

"When she passes, I think, *I will never see a lady like this again*," he said. He had finally introduced himself.

Zenovia and her husband, Ignacio Ash, a Mayan organic farmer, raised crops two miles up, near the source of the Columbia River where cold water bubbled up from rocks. They practiced permaculture, a form of farming designed around the cycles in natural ecosystems and perfectly designed to appeal to Profilio's sensibilities.

He had started learning everything he could about their farm, but also studied them.

"They are fifty-fifty in everything they do. She's the only lady I know that loves her husband a lot. I want to learn so when we are old my wife will think of me as Zenovia does Mr. Ash," Profilio, who was picking up relationship goals with farming advice, told me.

I stopped to chat and learned Profilio was now insisting his sons learn to cook and he was doing jobs at the house that he previously considered woman's work.

I asked him if his wife loved him more.

"Yes," he said. "And me, her. We're fifty-fifty."

I had met Zenovia. On a tip from Alisa of Chaos Oasis, I had bought organic coffee beans from her at the market in PG. In true Alisa storytelling form, she had performed the tale of her first ride with Zenovia when the boat had been too overloaded with women returning from the market. The boat had sunk lower and lower until passengers were sitting in the water. The women had merely transferred their baskets to the top of their heads. I was looking forward to taking one of Zenovia's dory trips to the source of the river.

But the water level in the river was so low at this time that there were spots where you had to get out of the boat and walk in jungle.

"This is not good for your distaste of snakes," Profilio told me.

It hadn't rained lately, but it was still too early for the dry season to settle in unrelentingly. I'd get my chance.

I wandered down to the farm, poking my head in at the different houses to say hello. I caught Sebastian working on a schedule with a list of the employee names and asked him how he chose who to hire.

I don't want to sound cynical, but it seemed odd to me that every person on a staff of thirteen was dedicated, and most had been there for years.

At first, I thought Sebastian just hired family. But he was related to so many people in the village that it would only cut the pool of candidates by a little; plus, he did have some people on staff who weren't relatives.

Sebastian told me he watched potential employees for a very long time as they went about their lives in the village.

"Maybe a person is always mad at someone or someone is always mad at them," Sebastian said. "I think, *Maybe they will not get along well with the other workers.* Or maybe I see someone kick their bike or their washing machine because it's not working. Maybe someone like that gets frustrated and is rough. A person must be very gentle with butterflies."

Did he look for people with a passion for butterflies or conservation?

"It's not so important," he said. "I look for people who are calm and respectful of life."

I said that now I understood why Nestor worked at the farm.

Sebastian asked me, rather sharply, what I meant. I said that I just meant that Nestor was calm and kind, but when I talked with him, he wasn't as excited as the others about the larger purpose of the farm—it was like that old story about asking men cutting stones what they were doing: one said cutting stones, one said working to feed his family, and one said he was building a cathedral.

Sebastian looked at me with perhaps the most profound disappointment with which I have ever been regarded.

"I think I should tell you about Nestor," he said.

Nestor's father was not a dependable man, so Nestor's family moved around and Nestor didn't get to go to school very often. He taught himself, Sebastian said. So maybe when I asked Nestor questions in English, which in Maya Belize is the language of school and not home, he did not understand me well. Maybe he could not answer with his full thoughts.

Sebastian said Nestor was the exact opposite man of his father, always dependable. Even when he lost a child, the worst thing on earth, Nestor did not grow bitter or hard but loved his wife and the rest of his children double. Nestor had studied butterflies since he was a child. But before Nestor would accept the job, Sebastian had to convince him that writing was the least important part of the work, because Nestor worried that his spelling would make Sebastian's life harder. It was clear I'd been missing some things about Nestor, but also perhaps I'd been missing something about how Sebastian ran the farm. He didn't just care about the work. He cared about the workers.

About a week later, Moody and I were inside in the late afternoon when we heard the croak-croak of a toucan outside our window. That was unusual. We often saw toucans on top of the hill, but we had never seen one down by the house. There was another croak-croak. And another.

I didn't bother with my bug gear, just ran outside in shorts. Nestor had been coming up the path and had already stopped and was looking up as toucan after toucan flew in, then, after a while, flew off again. Moody raced down the stairs with binoculars, and the three of us passed them back and forth for about ten minutes watching a flock of some thirty birds with rainbow beaks make a quick stopover. They were likely heading to their nests after a big fruit-tree feast. This time, I noticed how Nestor's face was filled with quiet delight.

Seventeen

THE MOST DANGEROUS ANIMAL

The cohune tree's straggly starfish flowers turned to giant pods of seeds and then a carpet of polished brown nuts. In front of the blue morpho flight cage, a green iguana had laid her eggs in the sand. Anselmo said she was early.

For several days, temperatures had been rising and the air was abnormally still. For most of our stay, I'd had a running joke with the guys that when I met one of them on the steep zigzag staircase, I would say, "Have you ever . . . ," and they would say, "One hundred and fifty-nine!" before I added, "Counted the stairs?" But now we would stop and pant and blow our comic timing.

One day, Sebastian was on a ladder peering down into a black water tank. His face glistened with sweat and worry. "We have backup tanks, but this is too early," he said.

Before climate change took hold, there were predictable seasons in Belize. The rainy season was from June to November. The dry season November to June. The transition was soft: a tapering off of rain, a building heat. This season, it had gone abruptly from rain every night in January to no rain, and the air had a skin-prickling intensity.

That night, an electrical storm seemed to break directly over the house. Our room flashed brighter than from a house music strobe. The loud *cracks* emitting from the sky didn't seem in sync with the flashes. I waited for the drum of rain to interrupt, but it didn't come.

In the morning, Moody slept in for once. I couldn't sleep and, for once, got up early. I climbed to the top of the hill.

Sebastian, Bernaldo, and Profilio were silhouetted on the ridge, looking out. I'd witnessed enough wildfires to know that they were looking for smoke from lightning strikes. This time, we seemed to be in the clear.

The shift in temperature had brought an increase in the most dangerous animal in Belize, responsible for far more deaths than the feared fer-de-lance snake: mosquitoes, the world's most prolific vectors of disease.

I had already been dressing like an escapee from an REI photo shoot. Getting ready in the morning was a simple choice: either the khaki or olive safari pants and then either the white or terra-cotta or teal pragmatic long-sleeved, drip-dry hiking shirt. When going out the door, slide feet into snake-proof black rubber rain boots, add wide-brimmed hat, and, presto, ready.

I now added a bug-repellent lavender bandanna to the jungle-cruise look. But, still, I got bit. The mosquitoes found the air vents in my shirts. If I lifted my arms, and the skin below my shirt showed for even a second, stinging welts followed. They bit my eyebrows! Even if I was a fan of a slather of DEET, that wasn't a possibility on a butterfly sanctuary, as butterflies are sensitive insects too.

The bugs had been problematic from the beginning. On our day of arrival, unwinding with post-travel yoga, I put my hand down on a bright-blue bee. Despite the searing sting, I was fascinated by how my hand coming out of boat pose and the bee walking across the floor came to the same spot at the same moment. The bee seemed to be alright. It is only the poor honeybees that die from stinging a person. This iridescent bee walked a little farther and flew off. I had never seen a blue bee before.

Early in the trip, something bit Moody, and his hand ballooned up. It looked as if someone had blown into a surgical glove. He could barely bend his fingers. Profilio looked at it and said, "Oh, doctor fly. Yes, this is common. It's not a botfly."

At the time, considering how many things I was nervous about, the only thing I wanted to know about a botfly was that it hadn't bit Moody. It is only now, writing this, when I went to look up how to spell "botfly" (one word) that I discovered the scope of the grotesqueness.

A botfly attaches its eggs to a mosquito or fly, then when the mosquito or fly bites a human, the botfly eggs are laid headfirst under the person's skin. The person's body heat helps the eggs hatch. The larvae then feed and burrow. When they're ready to emerge, they turn around and crawl out.

Some of the headlines that pop up when one searches "botfly" and "Belize" are: "Mystery Wound in Honeymooner's Groin Was 'Deeply Embedded Maggot,'" "Burrowing Botfly Grows Huge Feasting on Your Flesh," and "Ten Most Terrifying Parasites Ever."

I strongly suggest you do not look at the accompanying photographs.

One afternoon, during the hot, heightened mosquito season, I tagged along with Marcellinus on his way to gather leaves for the blue morpho caterpillars. We went down a narrow trail I had not noticed before that led us into a wooded area. Marcellinus reached up high, pulling over flexible trees, then cutting them with his machete.

I asked if I could try. (It looked fun.)

"You'll get stung," he said, and I noticed the swarms of ants crawling over the branches.

"How do you keep them from biting you?" I asked.

He looked at me quizzically.

"They bite me," he said and held out his arms in his short-sleeved T-shirt. He was covered with mosquito bites and ant stings. They didn't show as much as the Barbie-pink welts on my arms, but they were there, an acre of bumps.

While we talked, the mosquitoes were biting. Their latest iteration, be it a different stage or species, could bite through clothes.

With great effort, I held it together near stoic Marcellinus. But once we said goodbye, I ran back to the cabin like a cartoon character with its hair on fire. I threw myself into a shower to calm down my skin and my freak-out. Stepping out of the cold water, I wrapped myself in a towel and went to brush my teeth. I pulled open my toothbrush holder and out streamed hundreds of tiny black ants. I screamed and threw the plastic case, hitting a spiderweb.

I felt like I was having a panic attack. I might have been. One theory is that your body releases histamine in response to a bite, setting off the itching reaction. When your histamine levels are too high, there is a natural release of adrenaline to counteract the histamine. Adrenaline can make your pulse race. They've also found high levels of histamine in the bloodstreams of people suffering from schizophrenia.

All I know was that I was stinging and itching and feeling bugs crawl on me even where I could see no bugs.

I sat in the middle of the bed and took deep breaths.

When Moody rushed in (he'd heard me scream), I told him that it was only me throwing my ant-covered toothbrush but asked him to look me over and tell me if he saw any bugs.

"No bugs," he said. "But you have a ton of bites. Wow—look at the size of that one!"

"I still feel bugs crawling all over me," I said.

"You haven't taken LSD?" he joked.

I told him that was my next move.

But, instead, we drove to Hickatee and I had a Gin-Gin with Alli.

Eighteen

Disc Brakes and the Bluest Butterfly

Moody and I had done a poor job of downloading entertainment for our trip.

Because of this, we had only one TV show. It was about the British monarchy, and we had taken to comparing everyone to the House of Windsor.

Alli was being cast on this day. She had been promising to explore Belize with us, but she always found more work she had to do first. I wanted her to take a day off.

"It's like you're Prince Philip trying to convince Queen Elizabeth not to visit fifty-seven towns and cities in fifty-eight days," Moody said.

"No," I said. "I am Prince George, who will send her on safari. Except my lungs are fine and I'm going too."

Alli finally scheduled time for a day trip. Moody told her she got to pick the destination. She chose Pine Hill, the Mennonite community in Toledo that none of us had ever visited.

The day of our outing, the sky was poster-paint blue with a block print of feathery white clouds. It was only hot. Not hot-hot-hot, and, for this, we were grateful.

Alli was feeling carefree and decided she was going to give the boys the option of ditching school and coming with us. Her guess was that

Jorge would turn her down. He was older and took his academics seriously. But she thought Little Eduardo would bite.

Sure enough, she came out of the school having sprung her youngest. Little Eduardo, with his freckled nose and orange-red sneakers, was always in motion. He was either trying to raise rabbits or plant a garden or crawling around looking for a particular kind of lizard.

I'd asked him once what he had seen growing up in Belize. He made this list. Don't mind any spelling errors, he's ten.

trantulas
scorpians
milipeds
centipedes
cane toads
blue morpho
boa konstrikters
ferdilance
blue crabs

He explained that he didn't add the rabbits and guinea pigs he raised because they have those in Texas.

We all piled into the Jeep and drove about an hour north on the Southern Highway. When we turned off on the road to Pine Hill, I felt displaced.

There were gently rolling green hills, wooden barns, manicured fields, and windmills. It was as if we'd left the highway and entered rural Pennsylvania, but with a smattering of palm trees.

"Look at that!" Moody said, pulling over near two parked wooden buggies.

I was surprised he was so taken by them, as the Mennonites were part of the regular diversity of Belize and we often saw buggies in PG on market day, as well as men in suspenders and women in homespun long dresses.

He got out, bent down, and looked closely at the buggy's wheels.

"Yep," said former bicycle mechanic Moody. "Disc brakes. Top of the line."

Eduardo and I petted two horses that were grazing nearby before we continued on our way. We drove about three miles, past pretty farmhouses and cows, but saw no people. Alli had thought there would be a store or a community center, but if there was, it was well hidden.

The road ended and we turned around.

As outings went, it had been pleasant but uneventful.

Up ahead, we watched as a small cloud of dust was getting bigger. Moody pulled over to the side to let the horse-drawn buggy pass. But the buggy stopped.

The woman driving was neither young nor old. Her hands holding the reins were large and sunburned. She had brown hair parted in the middle, level brows, and a scrubbed face free of cosmetics, all beside the point. Her charisma wasn't tied to her appearance. It was her presence. She crackled with intelligence and curiosity.

I had been afraid she was going to tell us we weren't welcome on this property. But Elizabeth introduced herself, and we told her our names. Moody was on the side closest to the buggy, so he explained that Alli ran a hotel near PG and that he and I were from California. Elizabeth said she had little opportunity to speak English. The rest of the women only spoke Low German. The men spoke Kriol and some English because they left the community to do business.

I was astounded that we had crossed paths with the only woman here who could talk with us.

Moody told her he couldn't help but notice the buggy's brakes.

She gave a laugh. She said it made no sense to her. The idea was to eschew modern contrivances and rely on what they created with their own hands, but they all had these brakes that certainly could not be made in their shops. But what did she know? She wasn't from here. She had lived in communities in Canada and Bolivia that were more conservative.

It was the men, the elders, who wanted the brakes, she said. Was I right in thinking her tone was exactly the same as a woman from the American South giving a dismissive "bless their hearts"?

"Well, they're certainly high-tech," Moody said about the brakes.

"What's 'high-tech' mean?" asked Elizabeth.

Moody told me later that he'd been taken aback, realizing that this wasn't a lack of vocabulary but that a world existed where high-tech didn't.

He looked to me, his resident word person, for translation. But I was stumped.

Alli chimed in: "Faaancy," she said.

"Oh, yes, I understand," Elizabeth said.

The two young girls peeking shyly around her were nieces. They had bright-blue eyes, bright-blond hair, and didn't speak English. They were probably third- or fourth-generation Belizean born.

The Mennonites came to Belize in 1958 and were closely tied to the birth of the nation. It was a time of rising anti-colonialism. George Cadle Price, the architect of Belize's peaceful revolution, who would become the first president of an independent country, was negotiating self-rule. A sticking point was how then British Honduras would feed its own people. The population was a hundred thousand at that time, and most people worked in industries controlled by colonial powers or practiced subsistence farming.

In the meantime, Mennonites needed to move again. A Christian sect dating to the reformation, they are strict pacifists who believe in living apart from the world—including governments. So they have a long history of having to migrate.

The Mennonites who first came to Belize trace their roots to Flemish people who moved to Russia and Prussia in the seventeenth century, then later, when Russia demanded military service, moved to remote regions of Canada. After World War I, Canada considered requiring military service and that Mennonite schools teach in English. The traditionalists moved to the Mexican state of Chihuahua. But in the late fifties, Mexico wanted the Mennonites to contribute to their social security program and possibly be eligible for a draft.

Price, the premier of what was still British Honduras, met with leaders of that Mennonite community. They reached an agreement. The Mennonites would provide large-scale agriculture—their expertise. The colony would sell them farmland for three dollars an acre, let them practice their religion free from persecution, and promise that their children would never serve in the army.

The Mennonites were now about 4 percent of the population in Belize. Different Mennonite communities had different cultures, with varying levels of modernity. All the cheese and yogurt and ice cream we bought was from Western Dairies, a Mennonite company in the north, and it was not delivered by buggy. But Elizabeth's community had obviously held tightly to the creed of being in the world but not of it.

After we said our goodbyes, on the drive back to modern Belize, Moody, Alli, and I talked about how much we had been taken by Elizabeth's friendly but commanding presence. Little Eduardo said, "She seemed really sure of herself."

He had put his finger on it. Elizabeth exuded the confidence of someone who felt sure of her world and her place in it. She had seemed as interested in talking to us as we were in talking to her. She had mentioned she lived with her mother in the house by the two big banyan trees.

It wasn't much as far as directions, but I'd taken note. I wanted to talk to Elizabeth again. If she were willing to share, I was dying to know more about her and the journey that had brought her to Belize.

But I wouldn't get the opportunity anytime soon. We were leaving for California. The decision had come quickly and seemed inevitable.

"I'm worried about using water," Moody had said a few days before.

"Me too," I agreed, frowning at the lack of Benadryl left in the tube I was squeezing onto fresh mosquito bites.

The unspoken question hung in the air: "Is it time to leave?"

Clive had written to say he couldn't come for at least another month. England was exiting the European Union, a decision that was causing upheaval, including in the butterfly business.

Fallen Stones was already running on the backup tanks of water. I was still hallucinating imaginary bugs crawling on my skin because of the unrelenting itch of bites from the real things.

We had left our departure open-ended because we didn't know who we would meet or what would happen.

That night, the temperature barely dipped when the sun went down. Moody and I lay flat in bed, looking up at a Japanese paper lantern we'd put over the bulb for less torture-room wattage.

"Do you feel ready to leave?" Moody asked.

"No," I said. "Do you?"

"No," he said.

The problem was that we had no choice. We couldn't keep using water with Sebastian worriedly checking the tanks. We were from California. Who more than us could understand worrying about running out of water?

But we would return as soon as possible. Clive had already told us we were welcome to use the house at any time.

Maybe the weather would be odd and it would rain late in dry season and we could return by April or May.

I'd take Zenovia's dory to the source of the Columbia River. We'd finally see the blue iguana by the trash pile that we kept missing. Clive, whose letters were full of nostalgia for Fallen Stones, would come and we would all share a meal together on the balcony: a dinner party! I would visit Elizabeth.

In the meantime, I planned to go to England, visit Kari, and spend time at Stratford so I could better understand its symbiotic relationship with Fallen Stones. Then, maybe I would follow a pupa from Fallen Stones to wherever it finally landed to better understand the worldwide desire to see tropical butterflies. A Russian oligarch would be great. Or I'd settle for a butterfly making a cameo on a film set.

Every day in Belize had been a cultural lesson for me. Earlier in our trip, I had tried explaining our life to Sebastian, thinking he might also like a look at a world different than his own. I told him that our dogs, Murphy and George, took road trips with us and hogged the couch and we had left them with friends so they could have a beach vacation. I couldn't convince him that I wasn't joking.

Sebastian didn't like dogs or music (other than the Mayan harp) or wasting time, all of which I thought were litmus tests for my affection. But I somehow really liked Sebastian. I would miss him.

I couldn't resist teasing him, though. I told him we had to go home because we missed our dogs.

The week of our departure, I wandered down to the blue morpho flight cage. Sebastian was there. It was an overcast day, the sky was the color of cement. But the dull day made the blue morphos flash even brighter. They were active, whirling in loops and zigzagging circles. I tried to memorize the sound of dozens of flapping butterfly wings.

My eyes fell on the long sticks in the middle of the cage, the ones I'd spent time hanging those bright-green chrysalides upon.

I realized I had left something important undone.

"Sebastian!" I gasped. "I never watched a butterfly emerge."

He said it had been a long time since he had observed this. It happened most days, but you had to have the patience to wait and he was always busy.

I raised my eyebrows. He nodded. We stood side by side and waited.

There is a weight and heft to moments spent in anticipation. Your body seems to fold in on itself. You're playing with time: suspending animation while you do nothing but wait for something in the future.

Diana Marcum

I had zeroed in on one of the pupae that I thought the likely candidate because I could see the faint outline of a butterfly inside.

We stood still. I grew antsy. Sebastian was better at stillness than me. I may have even wondered if it was worth it. We silently waited for about twenty very long minutes, and then Sebastian nodded his head at a chrysalis behind the one I was watching. It was splitting open.

Just then, Moody came whistling down the path.

"I've got organic trash," he called. "Fruit peels for the butterflies."

"Come here, come here," I said. "We're watching a blue morpho emerge."

I thought it was unfair that he got to watch without waiting, but I was also glad he wouldn't miss this.

The bright-green pupa had become translucent. It had circular seams like one of those crescent-roll packages you open by banging it on the kitchen counter. You could see through the chrysalis that the butterfly was hanging upside down.

From the seam opening on the top, there emerged six legs, then the proboscis, the long tubular feeding part of a butterfly. The chrysalis split more and the body dropped out. It was the same shape as the now-pale-green chrysalis and had stripes the same shade. The butterfly's legs were attached to the empty shell. There were two long antennae. I thought I saw eyes and wondered whether they saw me. The wings were wet and crumpled like a piece of laundry that had been left in the washing machine, and they were tiny, smaller than the butterfly's body.

Slowly the wings began—"unfurling" is the wrong word, and it wasn't as consistent as inflating. The wings just seemed to breathe and grow, a little here, a little there.

The scientific name for a butterfly emerging is "eclosion." A botanical garden in Virginia calls it by poet Mark Nepo's term "the exquisite risk." Nepo was diagnosed with cancer in his thirties and writes about experiencing life fully while knowing a future is uncertain.

The butterfly released an unpleasant-looking liquid from the tail end. "Waste. Butterfly poop," said Sebastian in case I hadn't figured that out.

It contained the leftover liquid that the butterfly's body had pumped into veins in its wings. During this stage, the butterfly's wings have to hang down unimpeded. Once the veins are open, the butterfly pulls that liquid back into its body, and as the wings dry, those veins become stiff and provide the wings structure and shape.

We could clearly see the butterfly's head and body, and its wings had expanded enough to see the browns and corals, the blacks and creams, the eye pattern of a blue morpho's outer wing. I didn't know enough then to look, but if I had, I might have seen a tiny oval membrane with a dome on top like a fried egg that sits at the base of the wings. It converts sound waves. Butterflies have their ears on their wings.

For some five minutes, the butterfly hung there, its wings expanding. Other pupae were opening now, and several butterflies were in different stages of emerging.

This first butterfly, our butterfly, flapped its wings and flashed an indescribable blue. There is only one thing more dazzling, more iridescent, more blue, than a blue morpho butterfly, and it is a newly emerged blue morpho butterfly.

I will never forget that color.

Two days later, Moody and I carried suitcases packed with our clothes up the 159 steps. Bernaldo carried the ice chest up like he had carried it down. Sebastian and Profilio brought the empty suitcases that had once held books and toys.

Sebastian's eyes looked red. He really was sentimental. Then I saw Moody's face. It had that set-in-stone look he gets when he is trying to contain his emotion. His eyes were watery and he looked a bit panicked. Profilio wouldn't meet my eyes. What was I going to do with these men? We were going to be back in a few months.

Sebastian gave us an envelope as we were leaving. I opened it in the car. The first letter was very official. At the top, he had written, "Fallen Stones Butterfly Ranch (Ltd)," the address, and date.

> Dear Ms. Diana and Mr. Jack,
> On behalf of my staff here at Fallen Stones I take this opportunity to thank you for being here with us . . .

It was written in the same careful printing with which he'd taught me the names of plants and butterflies. He told us to take care of one another and to come back.

The other piece of paper was a list of English translations of Kekchi phrases. I had almost forgotten that I'd asked Sebastian if he would write down some words for me. Written Kekchi is not widely standardized. I had asked him to just do the best he could. We were coming up to the Lubaantun sign, so it seemed the perfect time to read them:

From Sebastian Shol

Put it in your head—*K'e saha holom*
Put it in your mind/heart—*K'e sá ka'uuxl*
We are very happy in the time we are here together—*K'aja xsahitqachi ool naj wanqat ahi*

Now, I was crying.

We had told Sebastian and the staff to help themselves to our leftover canned goods and any other food in the kitchen. I had forgotten about the liquor we had left for Alli's bar at Hickatee.

We were at the airport when we started getting pictures of the party. They were up at the top. The sunset was beginning to add orange and pink stripes to the magnificent view. I was worried—they had to ride bicycles down that hill.

"Let them have their fun," Moody said. "It's too late anyway."

I watched more photos arrive as we waited at our gate. It was while we were boarding, just before I turned off my phone, that I got the last one. "Good God," I said to Moody. "Is that Sebastian dancing?"

Nineteen

ALONG THE WAY

Clive's House in the jungle didn't stay lonely long after we left. Sebastian was moving in as a last-ditch effort to save the farm.

By the time we reached California, the novel virus Moody had asked John, the store owner, about in January—the one he had thought wasn't a threat to his family in China because they did not live in Wuhan—was a global pandemic.

In San Pedro Columbia, it was eerily quiet. People didn't want to leave their houses. The Fallen Stones workers were afraid to go to work. There were only a few cases of COVID-19 in Belize at that point, but people had seen how numbers had spiked in other places.

Sebastian, at home in the village, and Clive, at his house in England, talked on the phone.

"All the guys are panicked. I'm scared too," Sebastian told him.

"Look after yourself. Look after the workers," Clive told him. "Do what you think is right."

Sebastian reduced the number of butterfly species they bred and worked with a skeleton staff. Alli helped the others fill out the forms for unemployment benefits and emergency relief the government made immediately available. The butterfly farm limped along, barely keeping breeding numbers of pupae.

I spoke to Clive on the phone. He was in lockdown at his estate and he sounded depressed. His financial manager had told him he could float Stratford and Fallen Stones with no revenue if he cut to the bare bones. She had suggested laying off Jane, the marketing director, because there was nothing to market. He wanted to wait.

In Belize, the country went into an emergency state. It's a young country in more ways than one. More than 40 percent of the population is under sixteen. This means the government provides services such as health and education to more people than work and pay taxes. The health system, such as it was, would crumble if there was a large virus outbreak. But almost 40 percent of jobs depended on tourism.

"Belize is in the fight of its life, for its life," the prime minister said in an address that crackled over radios throughout the village and announced a lockdown with people confined to their homes by threat of fine or arrest. No one was to be on the roads or travel without a permit. Not even to go to their family farms of corn and beans and cacao.

Sebastian and Clive spoke again.

"I think maybe this is the end, Mr. Clive," Sebastian said.

"You may be right, Mr. Sebastian," Clive said. "Try to keep breeding a few pupae in case we can begin again."

Sebastian decided he would move into the house, the same one where Moody and I had stayed, the one where Clive and Ray had philosophized, and he alone would bring the caterpillars and butterflies that were left to flight.

"I care about these creatures, and no one is coming to look after them," he told Hovita.

Sebastian was at his house packing rice and beans and a little of Hovita's chocolate for his spirits when Sammy showed up.

"I am coming as well," he told Sebastian.

They had moved all of the butterflies from the experimental branch next to Hickatee up to Fallen Stones as soon as the pandemic hit because, to get to the branch, David had to take a forty-five-minute bus ride from San Pedro Columbia to PG, pick up his bicycle at a local restaurant that had agreed to let him park it inside safe from thieves, and then ride three miles to the butterfly farm. And reverse the trip at the end of the day.

David showed up at Sebastian's house shortly after Sammy.

"I'm going with you," he told Sebastian. "You can't do this alone."

Did they realize that they couldn't come home for three weeks or more? Sebastian asked.

Sammy and David said yes.

"I got much happier. Maybe with three, we can keep production going," Sebastian told me on the phone. His voice came over clearly. I knew the best reception was at the top, so I pictured him standing by the flamboyant tree he had planted long ago.

"Hey," I asked. "How are you guys liking living with the bats?"

Sebastian said the bats were gone.

"I sprayed a little perfume that I think they might not like, and they left," he said.

"*What?* Why didn't you tell me about that when I had to pass bats to get to the snacks?" I asked.

"Well, I didn't know for sure," Sebastian said. "I just thought, *Maybe they won't like this smell.*"

It was the height of the dry season and very hot. The tanks ran out of water. Several times a day, Sebastian, David, and Sammy hiked to the trickle of a creek that had been the waterfall to collect water for the farm and carry it back in pails.

Alli drove through the roadblocks, which were manned by both the military and the police, to bring drinking water, bananas, rice, and beans to the farm. Even in a country of such diversity and near PG, where the mayor was Garifuna, Alli said she was 100 percent sure that she was always waved through because she is white. To help ensure her privilege, she always stopped at the little market in San Pedro Columbia on the way back down and bought juices and chips to hand out to the soldiers manning the roadblocks.

At the farm, their days started at first light, gathering leaves and feeding the blue morpho, the *Caligo memnon* (the owl butterfly), and the malachite butterflies. They counted eggs, tended plants, and hung pupae. Butterflies have short life spans. They picked up the dead butterflies before the ants came. They took a short lunch break and worked until dark each day, every day, without any days off.

Sebastian and David made fun of Sammy because he had lived his whole life with his mother and didn't know how to cook. They made him take his turn in the kitchen. They ate rice and beans and jipijapa—a plant they gathered from the jungle, the same one used for making those tourist trinket baskets that were invariably embroidered with "Belize" and a palm tree.

The three discovered what we had known well—the inverter made a horrible racket if you needed to charge a phone, and it charged faster if you turned off all the lights.

At night, they sat in darkness on the balcony. There were several wildfires burning around PG, and they could see the glow from the flames. They talked about whether Fallen Stones would survive.

One night, Sammy was exhausted and worried.

"What if we're just wasting our time here? What if there is no hope?" he asked.

David wasn't given to outbursts, but Sebastian suspected he was thinking the same thing.

Sebastian said his hope was to keep the caterpillars they had alive, then to hang their chrysalides and bring them to flight. Then do it again. He told Sammy that hope doesn't come all at once. If you don't give up, if you keep going, then maybe you find hope along the way. Anyway, they all had bills, and every day they worked was a day they were getting paid.

Sebastian actually had a plan in mind. But he didn't want to tell anyone until he knew they could pull it off.

Going into the second week, he didn't think they could. They were very tired. It was too much work for three. But he had it in his mind that his brother Marcellinus was going to come and help. He had not asked him. They had not talked. It was just, as he put it, "a thought in my imagination."

Marcellinus arrived a day later when Sebastian, David, and Sammy were cutting leaves for the blue morphos. He lived upriver. He'd bummed a boat ride in a friend's dory, hiked through Lubaantun, and came up the back way, skirting the roadblocks.

"Hello, I was worried about you. I came to help," he said and started cutting leaves with them.

The next day, they were feeding the malachite, the butterflies that Felipe, the one who taught me how to count butterflies' eggs, usually cared for.

Felipe walked in.

"Hello, I came to see my butterflies," he said.

Back in England, at Stratford, with borders closed and flight schedules interrupted all over the world, Sarka couldn't get the pupae shipped out in time from the last box Fallen Stones had sent. They went into the flight cage at the exhibit, which was closed like most everything in England, where virus cases and deaths were spiking. The new butterflies emerged. The butterflies already there were thriving in their solitude and populating in numbers greater than before. It was the most brilliant on-wing display Stratford had ever known. Tropical butterflies filled the air. Richard and James were the only ones who saw them.

At his estate in Dorset, Clive took long walks on the property he had restored with ponds and native plants. I pictured him in his bucket hat, with his gnarled, stout walking stick, passing his gnomes and the dream ladder.

He thought about what he had done with his life that really mattered to him.

"Being in lockdown made me realize how precious it all is and how we're destroying it and how much we all have to work to save it," he told me later.

People sometimes have a favorite quote that they turn to repeatedly in their life. Mine is: "Ice cream is a force for good in a morally ambiguous world." Source: anonymous, spotted in a Ben & Jerry's store circa 1993.

Clive's favorite quote, which kept repeating in his mind: "Wonder is the beginning of philosophy." Source: Socrates via Plato, passed on to him by Miriam Rothschild.

He decided that what he had in his life that mattered, other than his family, was Stratford and Fallen Stones. He was a savvy businessman who believed in profit. He had interests in different businesses in England, Switzerland, and the United States. The Stratford butterfly exhibit and the Belizean breeding farm were the worst bets in his portfolio. But he decided they were his priorities. If he ended up having to rob Peter to pay Paul—they were Paul.

It came back to wonder. He had been seized with a fascination for butterflies since childhood. It was an intrinsic mesmerization, an addiction to their colors and complexities.

He was the first to open a butterfly house as a major attraction. He thought it was a selfish business interest that allowed him to indulge his passion. Many other butterfly houses followed his lead. Millions of people have seen live tropical butterflies flying instead of carcasses under glass.

The way Clive thought about it on his soul-searching walks was that each of those people who marveled at a butterfly had an opportunity for wonder.

"When you feel wonder, you start thinking: *What is this thing exactly? How does it work? What's its part in the world? What can I do to help it survive?* You look at the world differently, and it accumulates," he said.

He began to sound hopeful, sending me updates on Stratford from his home in Dorset. The butterflies and plants were flourishing. Jane sent reporters updates on the butterfly house, and there was a steady stream of attention. People wanted butterfly news. Other parts of the world had more relaxed restrictions than England, and Sarka and James received queries from customers desperate to buy pupae because they were still open, and what good is a butterfly house without butterflies?

Sarka called Sebastian to see if he had any pupae that he could send.

Sebastian had been waiting for this day. He told her he had one thousand pupae. It was a full shipment.

He had ramped up production when Marcellinus and Felipe arrived and slowly brought back Nestor, Santiago, Malvin, and Bernaldo for three-day weeks. Julio and Anselmo stayed with their personal farms. Profilio got a promotion to the butterfly cages. James and Sarka worked the phones and sold every chrysalis. Alli worked the limited flight schedules and found a way to ship the box.

The money from the Belize livestock covered some of the losses at the gate in England. They were still in business. They could hold on for more than a year. Clive was certain that Stratford and Fallen Stones would survive. He wanted to make improvements while they were closed. He was imagining more plants, new butterflies, and everyone and their grandmother lined up to see them.

Twenty

UNCERTAINTY

In California, Moody and I arrived home at the beginning of March 2020, which we didn't realize would be an infamous time.

I had wondered if the COVID-19 threat might slow down our entry into the States. But we'd wound through security in Texas without any screenings. The only sign of caution that I noticed was one fellow traveler wearing gloves in the heat. At the Portland airport, I had noticed two young women wearing masks and had given them a wide berth, foolishly thinking they were ill.

There had been a mild worry in the back of my mind like the drumming of fingernails on a table. Not about us. I figured we'd be safe in rich America. But I was worried the virus could devastate tourism-dependent Belize.

Alice, the friend who Moody and I had snorkeled with on a perfect ocean day, is married to Ben, a jazz musician who had a concert the weekend of our return. I was looking forward to it. I would see Alice for the first time since Belize, as well as many other friends.

Ben remembers the band trying to decide what to do as news about the virus grew louder. Much of it Moody and I were unaware of. We had driven from Oregon, dogs in the back seat, choosing back roads and taking our time. You might be surprised at how much of rural California doesn't have a cell signal.

The keyboard player in the band said he was from Viking stock, and he thought they should fight on. The tabla player was a pharmacist, and he said he knew how pandemics worked and it would be morally and ethically wrong for them to bring people together when they could get sick. There was no direction from any authorities.

They canceled. I always associate my first personal awareness of the pandemic with music I didn't hear and friends I didn't see—tiny losses in comparison to the griefs people would come to suffer. But all the tiny losses added up to life the way it was, suddenly gone.

I walked down to the salon to get my wild jungle hair tamed. Uni, the stylist, was a friend, and Alice and most of my other girlfriends were her clients as well. Uni looked worried. Her husband was a Las Vegas tour guide for groups from Korea. Tourism from Asia had halted. The guides were gig workers who largely made their money in tips. Her husband was suddenly out of work with no severance pay or unemployment benefits.

A couple of hours after my haircut, Uni dropped in at my house. The shop had closed. The owner told everyone to go home. Then the landlord at her house called (Uni split her time between Fresno and Las Vegas) and told her she needed to move out of her rented room immediately. The landlord was older and worried about the virus. Uni had her car packed. She was leaving.

Moody thinks it's odd that I stock our cupboards with food as if I were some modern-day Scarlett O'Hara vowing to never go hungry again.

But with Uni there and a crisis becoming clearer, I ran around throwing shelf-stable groceries into bags and forcing Uni to take them. She and Moody thought I was overreacting. I hoped so.

On March 19, California went into lockdown, the first state to order everyone to stay home. Other states followed. By then, the hospitals in Italy were overrun and the stakes were clear.

At our little house in Fresno, I felt lucky because we had a yard. I worried about Jordan. Her ritzy digs in Miami had become something more like a prison. The communal areas were closed. The only outdoors she could reach without an elevator ride was her small balcony.

She wondered if the horrible flu she had told us about, the one she'd caught on a European ski trip, was actually COVID-19. She had stayed near a resort that had hidden an early breakout.

I went on long walks, and when I saw neighbors I knew, I shouted a hello from a distance and asked how they were.

"Can't complain," they'd often say, even the ones who had troubles. The words had a twang. In California's Central Valley, speech patterns are still influenced by the refugees from the Dust Bowl who settled here in the 1930s.

"Can't complain," I would say to myself as a reminder.

I toured my urban neighborhood as if I were Clive walking his grounds. I nodded approval at a beehive in a split tree at the end of the block. I turned over leaves on the lantana outside the dance studio, looking for caterpillars.

I took in the clouds against the Sierra, the magnolia tree in bloom on the corner, the multicolored bark on the crepe myrtles, and loved them all. I was getting as sentimental as Sebastian after two beers.

I also loved the mosquito-infested jungle that scared me, and our friends on the butterfly farm who were cooking up palm fronds for dinner. They kept sending worried texts, asking about us. In Belize, the government had closed the borders and sent workers home, offering unemployment benefits. By the end of March, their country had reported two cases; by the middle of April, they had eighteen. The United States reported over six hundred thousand cases in April, and people were standing in food lines. I'd had a false confidence in America.

I told them we were fine, and we were—the lucky ones who didn't have to go to a workplace or worry about food. Still, the threat I had internalized from witnessing drought and fires intensified. I had grown up in a church that I hadn't given a thought to in ages. But they'd been big on predicting the end of the world. Now, I found the checklist imprinted on my mind as a child was still there: drought, fires, disease, false leaders, and this was California, so the earthquake had always been coming.

Moody called me Polly Prepper when the hand-cranked radio with an SOS signal and candles arrived. But he got busy and refilled our supply of emergency water.

I thought about my grandmother, who was born Irene Patterson, a tiny Irish woman who took pride in her well-seasoned cast-iron frying pan and spotless floors.

She had a hard life. My grandfather was not a good man. My grandmother and my mother and all her siblings suffered his abuses. I was probably twelve when I asked my grandmother why she'd married him. She told me all her people had died in the 1918 flu pandemic. She was the only one who'd lived out of her large extended family. She was a fourteen-year-old orphan with no one else to turn to when she met my eighteen-year-old grandfather. She showed me the one photo she had of her parents.

I worried the pandemic would set adrift other people like the girl my grandmother had been.

I was supposed to be writing a travel memoir. But I couldn't travel. Flying was risky, borders were closed, and the butterfly farm the book was to be largely about wasn't sure to survive.

One day, I was in the bedroom cleaning out my closet because, yes, in the face of apocalyptic visions, I line up my shoes.

"I don't know what to do," I said, only realizing I'd spoken out loud when my dog Murphy swiveled his head around.

"I don't know what to do," I said again, closing my eyes like it was a prayer.

I thought of something my grandmother Irene had told me. It was in the context of house cleaning, a skill I'd never mastered, but wisdom translates to more than one subject.

"When you don't know what to do—do the thing in front of you," she had said.

The thing in front of me was my front yard. Janet, my horticulturist friend, had long railed about the damage wrought by lawns. It wasn't only the water and chemicals those perfect squares of green required—it was the plants that didn't exist for bees and butterflies. I wanted to fix our little square.

Moody liked the idea. He called a bunch of bicycle shops and picked up their used boxes. We put the cardboard over the grass. We had a truckload of mulch delivered. The pile of dirt was the plane tickets I hadn't bought, the restaurant meals we didn't eat, and the movies we didn't see. We spread the dirt over the cardboard.

The ancient Maya believed in cycles of destruction and creation. We would kill the grass and plant a butterfly garden.

I started writing this book. I began with when I'd first seen Fallen Stones and went from there. It became an escape. I liked going back in time when the big problems were lovers' quarrels and scorpions in the shower.

I kept the rabbit whistle that Catarino made on my bookshelf. It made me think that it's true that objects can carry spirits. When I glanced at it, I was filled with thoughts—or more like the feeling—of being at Lubaantun. But the whistle was more to me than a clay post-card. It was a little statue of encouragement as I sat scribbling while the world fell apart. Stories meant something in a time longer ago than I can fathom—the clay rabbit whispered that, even now, they still might.

I thought I knew how the book would end. In Belize, Sammy had started to breed his butterfly again. Even when the plane routes began running as normal, there wouldn't be a way to get them to Clive in the regular box. This butterfly's pupating time was four days, and shipments took a week.

By the time what I was writing caught up to real time, I expected the pandemic would be past and the world opened. I would travel to Belize. Put the pupae in my carry-on. (Not technically illegal since Fallen Stones had the correct licenses to export butterflies, right?) I would fly to England and take the pupae to Clive in Dorset, making sure he knew they'd come from Manuel "Sammy" Cal before visiting Kari in London—my friend who I'd been visiting the first time I met Clive and saw the butterfly house. But months passed, and the pandemic only grew worse. In May, Kari had planned to return home to Maine for lilac season, which she loved. She couldn't travel. The COVID-19 rates in both the United States and England were staggering, and her illness made her high risk. I didn't dare think "next year." It made me feel like I was waving my face in front of a cobra.

In the United States, the virus laid bare the inequalities that made Black communities suffer more sickness and death. During this fraught reckoning, a police officer killed a Black man, George Floyd, by kneeling on his neck for nine minutes and forty-six seconds while other officers watched and a crowd screamed at him to stop. There had been generations of abuse, but this time, something was different. Maybe because there was video or maybe because the inequality had become so stark in a time of suffering. Protestors took to the streets during a pandemic, including my friend Jeanne.

Where I live in Fresno is rooted in a racist past that created different sides of town for different people, so the casual crisscrossing that leads to friendships is still often divided. Fifteen years ago, Jeanne noticed that she had no close white friends, and, she has told me, she felt that gave her a limited view.

She's religious, so she prayed for a white friend. The next week, I met her while I was reporting a story. That weekend, my friend Barbara and I ran into Jeanne at a jazz concert and shared a table. Jeanne thought it was a sign and that God had doubled down with two white women to add to her inner circle, and we have all been hanging out together since then.

I called her one Saturday morning with a cooking question, and she was on her way to a protest in downtown Fresno. She has had breast cancer and heart problems. I was worried that it wasn't safe for her to be in a crowd in a pandemic. She told me that racism was deadlier.

In the meantime, Moody's daughter, Kat, sent us a photo of a man in front of the courthouse in her small town holding a sign that said "Tyranny Sucks" about a mandate to wear masks in public places so people could protect others. It made me roll my eyes and laugh. Until men with guns and similar signs showed up in cities.

Alli had moved with her sons to Kansas City, Missouri, where Eduardo's company was headquartered, since she had no hotel guests in Belize. She sent photos of the family, masked at amusement parks and bowling alleys, which were still open in Missouri. I thought Little Eduardo looked panicked. I didn't think it was the mask. I was pretty sure it was because he'd rather be planting something.

Alli bought a ninety-nine-cent bright-blue notebook and carried it everywhere, jotting down ideas of what she could do to make a life in Belize again.

"It's our happy place. There is nothing glamorous about it. But we're part of a community there that we cared about," she wrote to me.

She and Eduardo are usually the inverse of me and Moody: Eduardo wants to have long talks. Alli usually just wants to get things done.

But now she was telling him her ideas. She wanted to ditch traditional tourism and re-create Hickatee in a way that would bring in only people who were there to help the community or the environment.

Just before she had left, she received her Belizean residency. To her, that red wax mark was a talisman. She was determined to return "home."

At Fallen Stones, the butterflies were flourishing. Sammy, a messaging fiend, kept Moody and me well supplied with emojis and snapshots of butterflies.

The dry season there passed, and it finally rained. Then, at the beginning of September, a hurricane formed in the Atlantic headed directly for Belize.

Sebastian had the crew take pupae from each of their species and put them in a box under a shelf with rocks on top before they all left to board up their houses.

I couldn't reach Sebastian that day. I called Sammy. There was high-pitched chatter behind him.

"What's that noise?" I asked.

"Oh, those are the chickens," he said. "The hurricane is beginning to hit, and I think they don't like rain."

The hurricane was named Nana, a ridiculously warm and fuzzy appellation for a destructive force. But also, hurricanes are named alphabetically, and it was unheard of to already be in the *N*'s in early September. (Two weeks later, meteorologists ran out of letters of the alphabet, there were so many storms.)

Nana destroyed banana crops in the central part of Belize. It missed Fallen Stones and the village.

I had sat in our house alone, watching the weather map and the blip that was a hurricane move toward the butterfly farm. Moody had left on his annual fly-fishing trip to his favorite place in the world, a river in southern Oregon where there are pine trees and vine maples and a yearly run of steelhead. The Umpqua River is his sacred ground. He took shaggy George. Murphy can't go on fishing trips because he jumps in the river and scares the fish and infuriates the fishers.

The night before Moody was to come home, a storm whipped and howled through their campsite, knocking down a tree that blocked him and his brother from leaving. A guy in a little Honda happened by. He had a big chain saw with him.

He cut up the tree, and as they were thanking him, a ranger drove up and yelled to everyone to evacuate immediately. Smoke suddenly poured over the ridge.

Because of the man with the chain saw, they could get the vehicles out. Moody drove home, zigzagging and rerouting for two days. There had been thousands of lightning strikes in what meteorologists called a siege. They hit landscapes that were dried by a scorching summer and the drought that ended in 2017. Wildfires burned out of control up and down the West Coast.

Instead of watching a blip of a hurricane on a computer screen, I checked road closures and fire fronts. Moody sent me a photo of a burnt-orange sky as dark as night. He'd shot it at noon.

When he reached home, George ran around in circles barking for ten minutes, and I hugged Moody almost as long. I waited to tell him that the mountains near us were also on fire. The trees were stressed by drought and bark beetles. They exploded. These aren't like the fires that are part of the natural cycle in California where the trees survive and the undergrowth comes back in spring.

Moody is usually semi-law-abiding. But he once dug up a sugar-maple vine near the Umpqua and brought it back and planted it in our backyard.

He kept staring at it.

"What if it's the only living thing left from there?" he asked.

My friend Shellee is a teacher to thirty-two third-graders from mostly farmworker families. She was trying to instruct them over their spotty Internet connections as they crowded on bunk beds or hid under a table for space. Each week, more of them turned off their cameras and she could not even see their faces.

Shellee had taken to leaving phone messages, with her saying only "It's going to be okay" in a weird, tense voice and then laughing maniacally.

"The world is blowing up," I said to Moody, the only person I still saw.

"It needs to," he said.

The only thing I could see on any side was uncertainty. I was clinging to that uncertainty as the closest thing to hope that felt true.

Climate change is warming the ocean and creating stronger storms. Fallen Stones could get hit again. It was only the beginning of fire season in California—if there was anything left to burn. The latest manifestations of the Ku Klux Klan were marching in American cities. COVID-19 was on its way to killing more than three million worldwide.

But there was still uncertainty.

Doom was not a foregone conclusion. Butterflies still dazzled. Some forests still grew. Friendships held. Perhaps Sebastian was right. Maybe hope is something you find along the way when you just keep going.

One day, when I was particularly overwhelmed with the state of the world and how to write a travel book when I couldn't travel, Moody went out and came home with ice cream: a force for good in a morally ambiguous world.

He also brought a chocolate cake. He'd given the bakery a photo of a blue morpho butterfly and had them draw one with frosting. He made a heart around the butterfly—with raisins.

Janet was going to help Moody and me plant. Gardening can be done from a safe distance. Janet and I first met when she was a fifteen-year-old waif in peasant skirts and sparkly ballet slippers and I was a seventeen-year-old who thought no skirt was too short as long as you paired it with an oversized off-the-shoulder sweatshirt. We came from backgrounds where the odds of us getting the bigger lives we dreamed of were slim. Yet, we've had our moments.

There was dirt waiting in my front yard. Janet was working on a garden plan. The health department was warning everyone to stay inside because of the smoke from the wildfires. But once the air cleared, we were going to grow host plants for eggs and caterpillars, and nectar-rich flowers for butterflies. Drought tolerant, of course.

It was a small thing. But those butterflies could be my brilliant, cosmic Post-it Notes. They could be reminders of how much beauty there is left and to do anything to save it. Put it in your head: *K'e saha holom*. Put it in your mind: *K'e sá ka'uuxl*.

HOW TO PLANT A BUTTERFLY GARDEN

By Janet Sluis, Horticulturist

For our lives to be filled with small, winged animals, we might need to adjust our expectations of what a yard is supposed to look like. There's a $40 billion industry set on making us equate grass and precision with respectability. Instead of an aesthetic based on European aristocracy, aim for more of a nature park vibe and less mini–*Downton Abbey*. The idea that every blade needs to be mowed, branch chipped, bug sprayed, and leaf blown into the neighbor's yard is not compatible with nature. Nature is messy. Nature does not make the bed every morning. Instead of sterile, fake meadows, think about creating a thriving, humming ecosystem that sustains life.

If you don't have a yard to plant in or aren't ready to give up your lawn, you can still help. Plant pots with herbs and let them go to flower. Even a small patio or balcony can support a substantial butterfly garden.

The first thing to do is to learn about *your* butterflies. Don't be tempted to rush out and buy an all-purpose butterfly garden kit, because it won't work. It's a huge deal to choose plants for butterflies specific to your region, and plants that will thrive where you live.

Fortunately, there are many fabulous resources for research, such as the North American Butterfly Association (NABA.org).

Choose a few butterflies you like that are also local to your area. Monarchs get a lot of attention, but they might not be native to where you live. Worldwide, there are 20,000 species of butterflies, 575 of them in North America, and many of them are in trouble.

Next, find the corresponding host plants. This is the most important step, since without the right host plant, butterflies will not lay their eggs. Alternately, you can pick from the list of host plants for local butterflies and just wait to see what shows up.

What if your garden is already full of plants? Now is a good time to take a long, hard look at each one. If you have plants that require annual applications of nasty insect-killing stuff, it's time to give them a shovel into the green waste bin. Same with plants that require excessive whacking to keep their shape, plants that are susceptible to diseases, or ones that just don't make you happy. Think of it as a closet cleaning. Out with the old so there is room for new things.

Most butterfly host plants are indigenous to the area where the butterfly is native, so this is really the area to focus on selecting plants that are native as well. Trees and shrubs are often overlooked but are arguably the most ecologically important plants to add. Butterflies need sturdy plants to provide shelter from wind, and some shade to hang out in on hot days, so look at placing a few native trees or large shrubs to provide both. In hot climates, midafternoon sun is so baking hot that you, your plants, and all other living creatures will appreciate the shade trees provide.

For smaller-scale host plants, the goal is to provide caterpillar food—plant enough for a small army. Nothing is worse than having hungry caterpillars. Half-munched plants might not be the most attractive focal point in your garden, so if you don't want these front and center, try hiding them behind other plants, or place them in areas that are not in your main line of sight.

After your larger plants are in place, scatter a few rocks, ceramic pots, or decorative objects that can retain heat. Butterflies appreciate a warm spot to sun themselves, especially just after they emerge from their chrysalis. This is also a way to add color and interest to your garden.

Once your host plants and habitat areas are set with shade and caterpillar food and a nice place to sun, it is time to fill in the blanks with flowers that will provide nectar (aka sugar) for food. As tempting as it may be, now is not the time to rush out and buy one of everything blooming at the nursery.

Think in seasons (late winter to early spring, late spring to summer, and fall). Make sure to have enough blooming in each season to keep the butterflies well fed. I recommend sticking to a specific color palette—otherwise, things can get too visually chaotic. Personally, I like purples/ violets/ blues, white, and yellows, with a few red accents. But use this as an opportunity to get in touch with your inner artist. Butterflies like an assortment of flower forms, and love ones that have clusters of many smaller flowers (like lantana or butterfly bush), or that have a nice large landing pad in the center (à la the Shasta daisy). Butterflies need to be able to find their food, so it is best to plant these sugar sources in larger groupings (usually odd numbers work best, so three, five, seven, nine) of one plant. Aim for about a three-by-three-inch patch of each flower, ideally in three or so different spots in the garden. Choose a plant you like that blooms in each of the three blooming time frames and repeat until you run out of room.

Then channel your inner child and add some mud puddles. Birds, bees, and butterflies all need a water supply, and will leave a perfectly nice garden in search of it. Take a small, shallow dish or pot saucer, place a cup of soil in it, add a few pebbles or marbles (so they won't fall in and drown), and fill with water. Minerals found in soil will leach into the water, and then get sipped up. Refresh weekly.

Ditch the pesticides and chemicals. *All* of them. *Immediately.* You don't want to lure butterflies to your beautiful smorgasbord only for them to find it's laced with poison. Watch out for fertilizers with added "insect control," especially anything systemic. Use organic mulches, compost, and fertilizers. When possible, start your own flowering plants from seed (especially milkweed). This way, you know they have not been sprayed, and you can grow a lot more plants for your money.

Sit back and relax. Stop cleaning up the garden beds, and let old flowers, leaves, and the eggs hiding on them overwinter in place. Allow flower heads to set seed and provide much-needed winter food for birds. Let leaves accumulate on the ground, or move to a pile on-site, where they will break down to feed the soil and the worms. The annual fall garden cleanup routine is throwing out eggs, chrysalis, and hibernating beneficial critters.

Enlist the help of friends and neighbors by sowing extra seeds and give small pots away for planting. My neighbor and her granddaughters sowed pots of milkweed and put them out on the sidewalk with a "Please Take Home and Plant" sign. They were all gone by the end of the day. Remember, butterflies *fly*—the world is one big yard to them.

Get involved with your local parks, municipalities, and open spaces. Encourage them to plant more native host plants and regionally appropriate trees. In Europe, they are turning the sides of roadways, industrial park landscapes, and rooftops into meadows for butterflies and other pollinators.

You may be focused on butterflies, but nature is intertwined. Butterflies lay eggs that turn into caterpillars, which also feed the birds. Ninety-six percent of songbirds need insects (aphids, moths, caterpillars, etc.) for protein to feed their young. Plant a bunch of host plants for butterflies to lay their eggs on, and birds, too, will take up residence in your garden.

Do anything you can to add life to the space you can control. Every blooming plant helps. Nectar sources can be grown anywhere, on patios, balconies, rooftops on tall buildings, even window boxes.

Together, these steps might make a difference. Together, they might help rebuild an ecosystem.

ACKNOWLEDGMENTS

I have many thanks to express as well as wanting to sneak in updates.

In England the Stratford-upon-Avon Butterfly Farm re-opened in 2021. I want to thank Clive Farrell for his generosity with his time and jungle house, and for passing on the wisdom that it all comes back to wonder. I want to thank James Ship, Sarka Bohac, Jane Kendrick, and the rest of the crew at Stratford—as well as those at other butterfly farms and places of wonder—who found ways to hang on and be waiting for all of us when the world re-opened.

In Belize, I want to thank Sebastian Shol and the crew that was there during our stay: Marcellinus Shol, Nestor Hun, Felipe Choc, Manuel "Sammy" Cal, Santiago Coc, Malvin Chiac, Anselmo Ical, Julio Cal, David Coh, Bernaldo Shol, and Profilio Sanchez. This is your story. Thank you for teaching me so many things. Thank you for not getting mad when I slowed down your workday. Thank you for saving Fallen Stones.

Thanks to Alli Gonzales, who I hope is back in Belize with an open inn and a thriving socially conscious export business by the time you're reading this book. We became close WhatsApp friends as we muddled through the pandemic year trying to find our paths. Alli started a company called CoHune (www.experiencecohune.com) selling Belizean artisan crafts to help women in remote villages and build the community in Toledo. I thrilled at her every adventure as she explored and forged relationships.

I want to thank my editor Laura Van der Veer, for her intelligence, care, and the other things you would normally appreciate in a good editor—but more than that. During the time we were editing this book about resilience, Laura was the very embodiment of the theme. She contracted and recovered from COVID-19, was pregnant during a pandemic, then looked for a bigger place in NYC, which I gather is almost as challenging as the previous two, all with wit and fortitude. (Sure, she'd temporarily lost her sense of smell, but that meant she and her husband could cook fish in a tiny apartment! Why not finish editing this book and move in the same week?)

Thank you to Carmen Johnson, Emma Reh, Lucy Silag, Merideth Mulroney, and everyone at Little A who shepherded the book through production and to readers. And as always, thanks to my agent Bonnie Nadell for her smarts and support. It's a kick-ass group of women who make up my book world.

Thank you to my Fresno neighbors Patience Milrod, Paul Pierce, and Lynda Meyers, and to Simone Hunt in Belize, who read early drafts with such enthusiasm that they inspired me to finish. Thank you to Michael Mayhew for the kind of detailed, insightful feedback for which he usually gets paid. (Owe you lunch, man. I can't pay scale.) Thanks to Joe and Donna Mathews, who watched our dogs so I could watch butterflies. Thanks to Barbara Anderson, who read a late draft of the book and cried at the end which convinced me to hit "send." Thanks to Janet Sluis for writing the end.

Thanks to the rest of my circle of girlfriends who get me through good and bad drafts both in writing and in life, several who made appearances in this book, not all by their real names.

A special thanks to the extraordinary Kari Howard, eternal optimist, pragmatic New Englander, brilliant wordsmith, and believer in embracing all of life's lunacy, sorrow, and joy.

Thank you to Mark Crosse, aka the unflappable Jack Moody, who moved to a jungle with me and always says "yes" when I ask "Hey, can I read you something I just wrote?" I'm glad we're in this life together. I'm glad he's sitting on the other end of the couch as I write this.

I told him he gets to pick the next adventure. I'm hoping he's kidding about Antarctica.

ABOUT THE AUTHOR

Diana Marcum is the nationally bestselling author of *The Tenth Island: Finding Joy, Beauty, and Unexpected Love in the Azores*. A feature writer at the *Los Angeles Times*, Diana won the Pulitzer Prize in 2015 for her narrative portraits of farmers, field-workers, and others in the drought-stricken towns of California's Central Valley.